Personalizing Language Learning

CAMBRIDGE HANDBOOKS FOR LANGUAGE TEACHERS

This is a series of practical guides for teachers of English and other languages. Illustrative examples are usually drawn from the field of English as a foreign or second language, but the ideas and techniques described can equally well be used in the teaching of any language

In this series:

Drama Techniques in Language Learning – A resource book of communication activities for language teachers *by Alan Maley and Alan Duff*

Games for Language Learning *by Andrew Wright, David Betteridge and Michael Buckby*

Discussions that Work – Task-centred fluency practice *by Penny Ur*

Once Upon a Time – Using stories in the language classroom *by John Morgan and Mario Rinvolucri*

Teaching Listening Comprehension *by Penny Ur*

Keep Talking – Communicative fluency activities for language teaching *by Friederike Klippel*

Working with Words – A guide to teaching and learning vocabulary *by Ruth Gairns and Stuart Redman*

Learner English – A teacher's guide to interference and other problems *edited by Michael Swan and Bernard Smith*

Testing Spoken Language – A handbook of oral testing techniques *by Nic Underhill*

Literature in the Language Classroom – A resource book of ideas and activities *by Joanne Collie and Stephen Slater*

Dictation – New methods, new possibilities *by Paul Davis and Mario Rinvolucri*

Grammar Practice Activities – A practical guide for teachers *by Penny Ur*

Testing for Language Teachers *by Arthur Hughes*

Pictures for Language Learning *by Andrew Wright*

Five-Minute Activities – A resource book of short activities *by Penny Ur and Andrew Wright*

The Standby Book – Activities for the language classroom *edited by Seth Lindstromberg*

Lessons from Nothing – Activities for language teaching with limited time and resources *by Bruce Marsland*

Beginning to Write – Writing activities for elementary and intermediate learners *by Arthur Brookes and Peter Grundy*

Ways of Doing – Students explore their everyday and classroom processes *by Paul Davis, Barbara Garside and Mario Rinvolucri*

Using Newspapers in the Classroom *by Paul Sanderson*

Teaching English Spelling – A practical guide *by Ruth Shemesh and Sheila Waller*

Personalizing Language Learning *by Griff Griffiths and Kathy Keohane*

Personalizing
Language Learning

ık is tʰ ʰ ʰ ned on or befoʰ

Griff Griffiths and
Kathy Keohane

CAMBRIDGE
UNIVERSITY PRESS

PUBLISHED BY THE PRESS SYNDICATE OF THE UNIVERSITY OF CAMBRIDGE
The Pitt Building, Trumpington Street, Cambridge, United Kingdom

CAMBRIDGE UNIVERSITY PRESS
The Edinburgh Building, Cambridge CB2 2RU, UK
40 West 20th Street, New York, NY 10011–4211, USA
10 Stamford Road, Oakleigh, VIC 3166, Australia
Ruiz de Alarcón 13, 28014 Madrid, Spain
Dock House, The Waterfront, Cape Town 8001, South Africa

http://www.cambridge.org

First published 2000
Reprinted 2001

Printed in the United Kingdom at the University Press, Cambridge

Typeset in Sabon 10.5/12pt   [CE]

A catalogue record for this book is available from the British Library

Library of Congress Cataloging-in-Publication Data

Griffiths, Griff.
Personalizing language learning / Griff Griffiths and Kathy Keohane.
    p.   cm. – (Cambridge handbooks for language teachers)
Includes bibliographical references (p. 155) and index.
ISBN 0-521-63364-8 (pb)
1. Language and languages–Study and teaching.
I. Keohane, Kathy.   II. Title.   III. Series.

P51.G735 1999
418′.007–dc21   99–055435

ISBN 0 521 63364 8 paperback

To the memory of my father, Patrick Keohane

For

Janice
Fleur
Esther
Jesse

In hope of a second century
of love and friendship

How many things by season seasoned are
To their right praise and true perfection.
(Shakespeare: *The Merchant of Venice* V, i, 107–8)

Contents

Contents

Thanks and acknowledgements

This book is the result of the collaboration of Griff Griffiths and Kathy Keohane. Our on-going professional alliance, and the decision to work together to create a book of personalization activities, owe much to the enthusiasm for our ideas by the language teachers we worked with at the Berzsenyi Daniel College, Szombathely, Hungary. The activities in this book were further developed after we had stopped working with those teachers, and the finished product is the result of our own creativity combined with the influence of others; we have acknowledged them individually in the activities where appropriate.

We would like to thank Seth Lindstromberg for his initial encouragement of our ideas, Alison Sharpe for commissioning this book, Jane Clifford for her support, and Penny Ur for her outstanding editorial guidance.

The authors and publishers are grateful to the authors, publishers and others who have given their permission for the use of copyright information identified in the text. While every endeavour has been made, it has not been possible to identify the sources of all material used and in such cases the publishers would welcome information from copyright sources.

The authors would also like to thank Antony Seldon for the illustrations which appear throughout the book.

Introduction

This book provides a collection of creative classroom activities designed for busy teachers who wish to enhance language learning by integrating the personal experiences, feelings, values and opinions of individual learners into their classrooms. The activities are likely to be used as occasional enrichments to supplement your own course materials, adding a personally relevant dimension to otherwise impersonal textbook generated work.

The need for personalization: motivation and involvement

As language teachers, we are well aware that learners need to be motivated in order to be successful. Personal involvement is one very effective way of enhancing motivation. By this, we mean making language learning content personally meaningful. If learners feel that what they are asked to do is relevant to their own lives, and that their feelings, thoughts, opinions and knowledge are valued, and crucial to the success of the activities, then they will be fully engaged in the tasks and more likely to be motivated to learn the target language.

Textbooks, the core material for most classrooms, however, very often fail to achieve this level of involvement by learners. A great deal of commonly used material, particularly that used to model or elicit dialogue, is based on imaginary characters. Many listening or reading texts revolve around pre-selected topics which may have little interest for learners. Practice in particular language areas (e.g. grammar or pronunciation) is generally provided in exercises developed from these initial stimuli.

One example of a typical coursebook approach to the study of 'likes and dislikes' goes as follows. The language area is often presented or practised within the context of fictional characters who bear no relation to students' own lives. The lesson proceeds with students talking about what these imaginary people do and don't like, perhaps taking on the role of a specific character. A whole lesson could pass with only cursory reference to what the learners actually feel about things themselves.

There is no doubt that there are some learners who will be motivated regardless of the materials they use; there is also no doubt that many will not. There are always those who will fail to be inspired by materials which ignore their own world view. It is surprisingly easy, particularly when working with traditional materials, to neglect learners' individuality by omitting personally meaningful content.

The foreign language teacher is, however, in a position to enable truly interesting material to be used in class. The foreign language classroom has a flexibility unavailable in other subjects. Language learning aims can be achieved without teachers having to confine themselves to set texts or subjects. This being the case, the approach we advocate in this book is to take the learners themselves as the starting point for language practice. To stay with the example of likes and dislikes, learning is likely to be much more effective for far more learners if the teacher uses the students' own likes and dislikes (see 1.6) as the basis for an activity.

Specifically, we have found that our activities help in

- creating trust between class and teacher;
- facilitating positive group dynamics with your class;
- securing honest, helpful, and interesting feedback;
- bringing humour into the classroom;
- making language learning something you and your students will recall with affection;
- making language learning memorable.

Taking a humanistic approach

Some teachers have reservations about taking a humanistic approach. These teachers are concerned that they should not 'play the psychologist' in their classes; they fear they may delve too deep into their learners' personalities and they feel that the classroom may be the wrong place to do this. These same teachers may, however, feel that their classrooms need invigorating, their learners need remotivating and need to feel that the language learning class is personally relevant.

The activities presented in this book aim to involve learners' thoughts, opinions, knowledge and feelings with what they are learning without prying or making learners reveal what they would rather not. It helps to preserve individuals' right to privacy, and to create a feeling of trust in the classroom, if you make sure that learners know they will not be forced to participate; they should have the right to 'pass' in an activity. The activities do vary, from the mild revelations in 1.3 'Name round' to the potentially deeper discussions in 6.1 'My past, my self'. You yourself are the best judge of how comfortable you and your learners are with more revealing activities.

Teacher participation

We feel it improves the general atmosphere if you participate in the activities yourself. By participate, we mean that you should contribute in ways that are similar to how the students are contributing: if the students are asked to relate an important event from the past, the teacher should also do so. Unlike traditional activities, ours are eminently suitable for this. Everybody knows that the teacher can correctly complete a grammar exercise, but nobody knows what months were special to their teacher (see 7.6 Months in my life). Your participation should help learners to understand clearly what they have to do, as well as provide examples of appropriate language. In addition, we have found that this type of teacher participation has a positive effect on teacher–learner relationships, creates a comfortable classroom climate, and develops a trusting atmosphere between all participants.

Organization

The book is divided into eight sections as follows.

Chapter 1, 'Starting the course', provides opportunities for learners to talk to each other about themselves – who they are, what they are like, what is / has been important to them, what they like and dislike and their current attitude to the target language. As well as being used to begin a course, activities from 'Starting the course' can be used mid-course for a group that hasn't seemed to gel, or for a group starting a new academic year.

Chapter 2, 'Warming up', takes the ice-breaking a stage further. It looks at different topics and relates them directly to students' own lives. Learners are asked to think about particular places and events they consider important, to make careful observations of sounds and objects and to work collaboratively, finding out what they have in common with each other.

Chapter 3, 'Acting, reacting, interacting', is concerned with maximizing classroom opportunities for interaction. It contains activities which produce short narrations, student-generated dialogues, role plays, drama, and written interaction.

Chapter 4 is called 'Self-awareness and self-assertion'. All the activities in this chapter demand a high degree of interaction with others. There are three strands. The first, awareness of self, in this chapter means asking learners to think about what they are like in terms of physical appearance and personality, and to recognize their own qualities. This strand also asks them to think about themselves in terms of what makes them angry and what makes them laugh. The second, awareness of others, here means being conscious of how to deal with people in both straightforward and difficult situations. There are opportunities for learners to gauge the appropriacy of questions in specific contexts, to persuade in calm and emotional situations, to sympathize and empathize, and to avoid conversation in public situations. Self-assertion, the final strand, means, as well as being able to deal with others effectively in difficult and potential conflict situations, learning how to distinguish between assertive, unassertive and aggressive modes of speech.

Chapter 5, 'Values and values awareness', considers the emotional value of material things. It also provides opportunities for learners to think about what qualities they value in people and which qualities enhance their own enjoyment of life. Learners have the chance to think about how people's values are likely to be different depending on their role in life. In addition they are asked to think about their own values in a wider sense by assessing their willingness to contribute to a variety of different causes.

Chapter 6 is called 'Self-knowledge'. This chapter contains activities which ask learners to think about themselves in the past and present. Learners have the chance to think about what they used to be like and to use important, or simply memorable, past experiences for language practice activities. Activities in this section also ask learners to think about the things in their life which make them the people they are now – for example what they're good at, what they want from life and what's important to them, not only in terms of serious values, but also with reference to the small but important choices they make and preferences they have on a day-to-day basis that make them unique individuals.

Chapter 7, 'Images and scenes – real and ideal', has activities to describe, in speaking and writing, pictures of people and places. This chapter also asks learners to tell stories, inventing some and using real events in their lives as the basis for others. In addition, Chapter 7 provides opportunities to act out mini-dramas generated by learners' own experiences.

The final chapter, Chapter 8, 'Closing the course', does three things. It provides an opportunity for students to reflect on what the course and their fellow classmates have meant to them, suggests ways of eliciting useful feedback, and gives some ideas for leave-taking activities. Ideas from this chapter can also be used earlier in the course to elicit useful feedback.

The activities

Content

The process of individual activities is described briefly, with examples. For each activity, a specific language focus is provided, and an indication of the minimum language level required for the task. Any necessary materials and preparation are detailed where appropriate. Many activities have sample texts for teachers to use.

Variations

We often suggest additional different ways of doing the activities, which we have called 'Variations'. The function of these Variations may be:

- to refine the base activity to suit a particular set of learners according to group composition, age, level and class size (see 1.1);
- to alter the language focus – i.e. keeping the stages of the activity the same but looking at different language areas (see 1.6);
- to extend or limit the language focus according to level (see 3.7);
- to provide an alternative shorter or simpler activity (see 7.7);
- to provide something which you might prefer (see 3.1);
- to provide less intrusive alternatives (see 3.5).

Follow-ons

Similarly, you will find sections headed 'Follow-on' which broaden or add new components to the original activity. Some of the activities in these sections extend the language focus, introducing new points within the same area (see 1.8) or provide extra practice in, for example, question formation (see 7.7). Where appropriate, we have indicated follow-on activities aimed at a specific level (see 6.1) or a particular skill, especially writing (see 2.1).

Age and level

All the activities can be used with adults. The majority can be used with teenagers, and some are suitable for even younger learners. Where helpful and appropriate, specific variations are offered for non-adult groups. The instructions for each activity indicate its suitability for adults, teenagers or children through the use of subheadings.

We have, as mentioned above, included a recommendation as to language level in our preliminary definitions for each activity. However, the majority of the activities are suitable, or can be adapted for a variety of levels. Normally the students themselves determine the complexity of the language used. The character of the conversations which take place in Activity 2.2 'The parts of my life' will be very different with a lower-intermediate group and an advanced group, but the activity can be used successfully with both levels. For many of the activities we have suggested pre- or post-work activities, as described in the previous paragraph, which can also help to raise or lower the level.

Movement

Note that many of our activities necessitate movement by learners and teachers. Since most real-world communication entails both body language and mobility, we feel that this adds authenticity and individuality.

Pre-teaching

Note also that you may need to pre-teach specific vocabulary for some of the activities: for example activity 1.3, 'Name round', will not be successful unless learners already know the names of a variety of jobs in English. Activity 4.3, 'Empathizing and persuading', may fail if learners have an insufficient repertoire of persuasive phrases.

We hope and believe the activities in this book will enhance the atmosphere and motivation in your classes. They have achieved this and much more in the classrooms of the world where we have used them.

1 Starting the course

1.1 Multi-introductions

Introducing people in English

This is a very useful 'getting-to-know-you' activity for the beginning of a course

Language focus   Introducing people

Level   Elementary upwards

Materials   Board; slips of paper

Procedure

FOR ADULTS, TEENAGERS AND CHILDREN

1 On the board, write the following:

   Name   Favourite colours   Favourite pastime   Extra information

2 Write in information about yourself beside each area, for example:

Name:	Kathy
Favourite colour:	Red
Favourite pastime:	Walking
Extra information:	Passed driving test at 31

   Then ask the class to do the same on slips of paper. Explain that the 'extra information' section can include anything that they would be happy for other people to know about them, for example their zodiac sign, their shoe size, what they like to eat, somewhere they have been that they liked, etc. Elicit from the students more ideas of the type of thing they might include.

3 Ask one of the learners to introduce you as if the class didn't know you at all. The introduction might go like this:

I'd like to introduce Kathy. She likes the colour red and enjoys walking. Kathy passed her driving test when she was 31.

4 Divide the class into As and Bs. As are going to introduce their partner to someone else. Bs should give As the slip of paper to use as a cue if they need it.
5 With everybody standing in pairs, As approach another pair and both As introduce their partner. When both As have spoken, they exchange partners and papers and introduce their partner to another A. At the end of this, a new exchange takes place and so it goes on, with As introducing a new partner each time.
6 After about five minutes, As and Bs exchange roles.
7 At the end of the activity, collect all the slips of paper in. Read out the piece of 'extra information' and challenge the class to remember who it's about.

Variation

The activity can be easily adapted to suit specific groups of students by changing the headings. Make up your own or choose three or so from the suggestions in Box 1.

Box 1 Multi-introductions

Multilingual groups

nationality / home town / place of birth / native language / national dish / favourite famous fellow citizen

Adult

place of work / job / place of birth / favourite decade / greatest personal achievement / ambition

Children

age / good friend's name / pet's name / number of brothers and sisters / favourite toy / favourite non-school activity / favourite lesson

---

1.2 Personality descriptions

Describing yourself and others

This is also a good early-on 'getting-to-know-you' activity.

Language focus   Describing people
Level   Lower-intermediate upwards
Materials   Board; A4 paper

Procedure

FOR ADULTS AND TEENAGERS

Part 1

1 Write the following words on the board and ask learners to think about themselves in terms of these areas:

family, future plans, background, likes and dislikes, hobbies and pastimes.

2 Use these headings to tell the class something about yourself, as in the sample text below:

> My name is Mike and I am from the South of England. I am married with three children – two boys and a girl. We live in a house which is too small for all of us, so we are going to extend it. This summer we are going to take a holiday in the Lake District. In September, my eldest son is going to start a new school – he is not very keen on the idea. I like our computer and I love my car. I like going to work and I enjoy meeting friends. In my spare time I play rugby and badminton.

Spend no more than two minutes doing this. At the end of your talk, give the class time to ask you questions about anything you've said. For example:

> – Which town in the South of England are you from?
> – What are your children's names?
> – How old is the boy who is going to start a new school?
> – Why is your son starting a new school?

3 Pair the learners (As and Bs) so that they're facing each other. As have two minutes to tell Bs as much as possible about themselves using the areas written on the board as a guide. After two minutes, Bs have the chance to ask As any questions. Then they exchange roles.

4 When both partners have spoken, give each learner an A4 size piece of paper. They should write their partner's name at the top and then the main points of what their partner has said, with assistance from their partner if need be. Notes for 'Mike' can be seen below:

> – from the South of England
> – married with 3 children
> – having house extended
> – going on holiday to the Lake District
> – son starting new school in September
> – likes car, computer, work, friends, rugby, badminton

Part 2

This can take place either immediately after Part 1, or in a subsequent lesson.

5 With the headings still on the board, ask learners to do a walkabout, finding out as much as they can about other people in their class. Allow about 15 minutes for this.

6 While learners are mingling, display the notes made at stage 4 around the room, with the name folded back.

7 Invite learners to try and identify the person from the notes. They can write their guesses at the bottom of the paper.

8 Finally fold back the name and reveal the person's identity.

FOR CHILDREN

Follow the same pattern as for adults and teenagers but tailor the initial headings to suit the age of your class. These ideas can work well:

family, place you live, what you like and dislike about school, favourite toys, favourite holiday activities.

1.3 Name round

Recalling or stating personal ambition

Language focus Jobs / professions
Level Lower-intermediate upwards
Materials A4 paper for follow-on
Preparation Review jobs / professions

Procedure

FOR ADULTS

1 Ask learners to close their eyes and think what they were like at the age of 12. Give them enough time to really visualize themselves.
2 The teacher begins the round on the lines of *I'm Griff, and when I was 12 I wanted to be a pop singer.*
3 The first learner to speak states their own remembered wishes. *I'm Kathy, and I wanted to be a journalist.*
This continues, with each learner recalling their personal ambitions at age 12.
4 After all the learners have spoken, challenge them to remember (saying or writing) what fellow students have said, for example:

Griff wanted to be a pop singer.

Writing or discussion follow-on for upper-intermediate upwards

a Each learner writes the profession they say they wanted to be at age 12 as a heading at the top of an A4 size piece of paper. Below this they should write the headings

Advantages Disadvantages Desirable qualities

and then stick it on the wall.
b Starting with their own paper, learners walk around the room and write at least one adjective or phrase underneath the appropriate heading. The start of a sheet for 'pop-singer' might look like this:

Advantages	Disadvantages	Desirable Qualities
*well-paid	*long hours	*ability to perform in public
*become famous	*unreliable career	*good voice
*get to travel	*difficult for family life	*stamina
*have fun performing	*no private life	*strong personality

c At the end of this stage, the person who owns the job returns and reads the comments. They can then use this as the raw material for a piece of writing describing why they would/wouldn't like to become what they wanted to be at age 12. The same material can subsequently be used as the basis of an informal discussion.

FOR TEENAGERS

Many teenagers have no clear idea of what they want to be, but have a firm idea of what they don't want. In order to allow learners to say something important about who they are and their future, without asking them to pretend a career decision, proceed as follows:

Ask learners to choose a job they would definitely not like to do. The round would then follow the format:

Learner 1: I'm Zahra, and I definitely don't want to be a housewife.
Learner 2: I'm Joseph, and I'm sure I don't want to be a teacher.

and continue with each learner adding their own sentence. Learners can be challenged to remember what others have said.

Writing follow-on for intermediate upwards

a Before the round starts, learners write the job they say they definitely don't want to do as a heading on A4 size paper and stick the sheets on the walls round the room, or simply place them on their desks.
b At the end of the round, ask all learners to write a positive or negative aspect of the job they have nominated on their piece of paper. They should then move around the room and write positive or negative adjectives for as many of the other jobs as they can. A semi-completed sheet for the job of 'housewife' might look like this:

Housewife	
Positive	Negative
are your own boss	alone a lot
valued by family	unstimulating
in control of own time	lots of menial tasks

c When this stage is finished, the owners return to their job. The information on the sheets can be used to write a paragraph which describes why they would not like to do this particular job, despite some of its positive attributes. An example of the type of response you might aim for from an intermediate learner based on the work in stage b can be seen in the following sample text:

> Some people love being a housewife. They like to be their own boss and know they are valued by their family. They also like to be in control of how they spend their time. However, I think I would be bored alone at home. I need to be with people and I need stimulation from my work. I don't think it's very stimulating cooking and cleaning every day.

FOR CHILDREN

Children often have a very clear (if ever-changing) idea of what they want to be.

1 Either elicit (perhaps using pictures) or brainstorm a variety of jobs and write them up on the board.
2 Proceed with the name round as for adults, starting the round with a learner who has a very clear idea of the job they want to do, e.g.

I'm Dorletta, and I want to be a doctor when I grow up.

3 After everyone has spoken, challenge the children to remember what other learners want to be when they grow up.

1.4 **Personal introductions**

Self-description

Language focus   Learning / reviewing adjectives
Level   Lower-intermediate upwards
Preparation   Review or pre-teach adjectives

Procedure

1 Ask the students to think of an object they feel they can identify with. It could be anything, anywhere.
2 Ask them to think of three words to describe it. Help them if necessary.
3 Model an encounter by introducing yourself to a student, e.g. *Hello, I'm a slipper. I'm old, warm and comfortable.* Then circulate and each member introduces themselves to all the other members.
4 Sit and reflect whether the qualities of your object describe you. If they don't, modify them in some way to describe yourself. Then circulate again and, shaking hands, reintroduce yourself in the same way as the object. Kathy's modified version of the slipper is: *Hello, I'm Kathy. I'm not old yet. I think I am a warm person, and my life is pretty comfortable.*

Writing follow-on for upper-intermediate upwards

a On the board, brainstorm 'adjectives that describe personal qualities'.
b Ask learners to copy the following continuum.

extremely negative	neutral	extremely positive

0	10

and to arrange the adjectives from stage a on to this personal evaluation continuum. The results will vary from learner to learner.
c Learners now create another continuum with adjectives to describe themselves, if possible at all points of the line. Illustrate with your own. Griff's is:

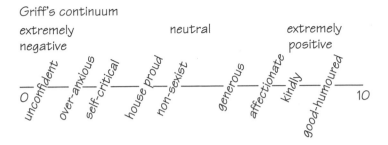

Griff's continuum

extremely   neutral   extremely
negative   positive

unconfident · over-anxious · self-critical · house proud · non-sexist · generous · affectionate · kindly · good-humoured

0   10

d Learners now exchange their continua with their partners and write a paragraph describing their partner's personality and expressing agreement or disagreement at the self-evaluation. The paragraph should end with some recommendations about how the weak personality points might be remedied. This is part of Kathy's written response to Griff's self-evaluation:

> What first struck me when I looked at your self-evaluation was . . .
> I'm not sure about the positioning of . . .
> In the main I agree . . .
> I am surprised to see that you consider yourself to be . . .
> Funnily enough . . .
> I think it's true that you are . . .
> There are two courses of action I can recommend to help you overcome . . .

FOR CHILDREN

Proceed as for adults and teenagers, but if you feel your learners would have difficulty with stage 4, or that it would make the activity tediously long, omit it.

1.5 Ask me a question

Looking at the familiar in a new way

This is like 1.4 in that it asks learners to identify with an inanimate object. The language focus, however, is different.

Language focus   Question practice

Level   Lower-intermediate upwards

Materials   Each learner must bring with them one object

Procedure

FOR ADULTS, TEENAGERS AND CHILDREN

1 Ask learners to bring a personal object of which they are very fond, e.g. a ring, book, soft toy, etc., to class.
2 Ask them to scrutinize and think about the chosen object very closely. They should focus on any wear and tear or damage, or anything that might indicate its use or history – how it was made, its shape, design, etc.
3 Now take the object you yourself like. Put it on a chair in the middle of the class or somehow display it prominently.
4 Sitting or standing near the object, introduce yourself as the object, e.g. *I'm a watch; I've been on my owner's wrist for three years; I was given him by a close friend. I was made in a big Russian factory.*
5 Now ask learners to ask questions of the watch, and you reply as though you were that object, e.g. *'Do you wish you were made of gold?' 'No, because I'd be more likely to be stolen.'*
6 Finally, ask learners to place their object in the centre of the circle, to introduce themselves as that object, and to field questions to the object.

Writing follow-on

a Invite learners to write a short biography of their chosen object, broadly using the chronological structure:

birth / early life / middle years / old age / life after death?

This sample text shows a short biography of a ring:

> This piece of jewellery began life as a small lump of gold. It was made into a Celtic ring. It was for sale in a small jewellery shop on an island. A man and a woman bought it when they were on holiday. It now belongs to the woman and she wears it as a wedding ring. When she dies, it may be buried with her.

b Display biographies on the wall for all to read.

Variation 1

Instead of a biography, learners can write an autobiographical account of their object as if they were the object. For example:

> I started life as a small lump of gold in Scotland and the man who owned me decided to make me into a Celtic ring. He hammered special designs on me and then I was ready. Then he put me into a box . . .

Variation 2

In some classes you might like to give the learners the chance to use a sketch of a favoured animal or pet.

1.6 What I like

Revealing your individuality

Language focus   Expressing likes and dislikes

Level   Elementary upwards

Materials   Board; slips of paper for follow-on

Procedure

FOR ADULTS, TEENAGERS AND CHILDREN

1 Write lots of 'things' on the board which are not obviously good or bad but which some people like and others don't. This can be an eclectic mix such as travel / aeroplanes / dogs / studying / flowers / sunshine / gold / TV / computers / hot weather. As you write, elicit ideas from learners.

2 Give learners a minute or two to choose the things they like best and the things they dislike.

3 The teacher starts and tells the class what she likes, what she dislikes, and says why. In an elementary class, this might go as follows:

I like dogs because they're good friends. I like flowers because they smell nice but I don't like hot weather because I feel very tired on hot days.

4 Now ask learners to do a walkabout activity, exchanging their information. Don't let this go on too long, but make sure everyone has a chance to speak to at least five different people.

5 When learners are seated again, ask them if anyone had any likes and dislikes the same as their own.

Variation 1

To review vocabulary, instead of 'things', brainstorm 'words' and ask learners to choose which words they like or don't like, taking into account sounds and meanings.

Variation 2

To review specific vocabulary areas (perhaps from your current coursebook) ask learners to say what they do and don't like about things from a particular lexical set such as 'clothes' or 'things in the kitchen', e.g. *I don't like toasters because I can never get the setting right.*

1.7 How I spend my time

Comparing real-world time constraints with ideal-world freedom

Language focus   Describing proportionate amounts of time

Level   Elementary upwards

Materials   Board

Preparation   Revise language to describe amounts of time

Procedure

FOR ADULTS AND TEENAGERS

1 Suggest learners create a life pie to show the ratio of time they spend on no more than six aspects of their life. This is Griff's life pie:

2 When learners have completed their own life pies, they should write an appraisal of how closely their actual life pie meets their ideal life pie. The resulting text will vary greatly between levels. These are examples of the type of language you might expect at three levels.

Elementary

I need to sleep less. I want to spend more time with my children.
I love listening to music but I can't do it very often.

Intermediate

Ideally I'd like to halve / greatly expand / reduce / abolish / triple the amount of time I spend on . . .

Advanced

In an ideal world, I'd spend the bulk of my time doing things which are relaxing and rewarding. This means that the amount of time I spend walking and with my children would instantly expand considerably, and . . .

Acknowledgement

We first saw life-pies used in Sheelagh Deller's book *Lessons from the Learner*. We first encountered the idea of using 'real' vs. 'ideal' from Peter Grundy.

1.8 Personalized greetings

Initiating and maintaining conversations

Language focus   Starting conversations and keeping them going

Level   Intermediate upwards

Materials   Large sticky labels

Preparation   Review ways of initiating and maintaining conversation

Procedure

FOR ADULTS AND TEENAGERS

1 On the board, write a few things that have happened to you recently. They should be the kind of things you would expect acquaintances to know about. Examples might include:

- an exam
- a holiday
- a house move

2 Review some ways of initiating and maintaining conversation. Examples of specific language for these can be found in Box 2.

3 After this review, give each learner a sticky label. On this they write three things that have happened to them recently which they would like to talk about. Once this has been done, they attach the label to them so that anyone can instantly see the three topics clearly.

4 A walkabout activity follows where learners greet each other and strike up conversations on one or all of the topics they have selected. It is a good idea to have a signal (for example, the blow of a whistle) to indicate when it's time to move on to another person. An example of the start of a conversation is shown below:

> A: Hi Klaus.
> B: Hello Saori.
> A: Have you had your oral exam yet?
> B: Yes. It was awful.
> A: Oh no!
> B: I said some really stupid things! And I made lots of mistakes
> – I know I did.
> A: Really? What a shame.
> B: I know. I'm hopeless at exams.
> A: Oh dear. Will you resit?

5 Allow the activity to carry on for no more than 15 minutes, with plenty of partner changes.
6 To round off the activity, when learners are again seated, challenge them to remember two pieces of information they were told during the walkabout.

Follow-on

This activity can be repeated and refined in subsequent lessons. Some work on subject changing and leave-taking may be introduced, with learners using specific phrases to initiate both.

Writing follow-on

a Give learners two dialogue openings, e.g.:

> A: Hello Ita, how's things?
> B: Marvellous. I've just found out I've won a competition!

> A: Hello Chie – all right?
> B: No, terrible – somebody stole my computer last night.

b Ask them to write a continuation of these dialogues. They should write at least four more exchanges, ending with a farewell.
c Display the dialogues around the room.

Variation for adults, teenagers and children

This is a much simpler 'greeting' activity. As set out below, it works only if students don't know each other's names. It can, however, be easily adapted for established classes if students choose new names for themselves. These might be English names, names they'd have liked to have if they could have chosen, or names of famous people they see as role models. It is particularly suitable for lower-level classes.

1   Starting the course

1 Ask participating learners to circulate and greet each other saying *Hello, I'm* . . . The other will respond *Hello, I'm* . . .
2 After everyone has greeted each other once, ask them to do another round; this time each tries to remember the other's name on the pattern '*Hello* . . ., *how are you today?*' '*I'm fine / OK thanks* . . . *How are you?*'

Note For lower-level learners in multi-lingual classes, remembering unfamiliar names can be very difficult. To make things easier, let learners wear name tags for stages 1 and 2.

Box 2 Personalized greetings

Initiating conversation	Maintaining conversation
Greeting:	**Empathizing: (negative)**
Hello!	Oh no!
Hi!	Oh dear!
Nice to see you again!	What a shame!
Long time no see!	How dreadful!
	How awful!
	That's atrocious!
Starting to ask questions:	**Empathizing: (positive)**
What's happened about. . .	That's good!
How's. . .	How nice!
Have you. . .	Excellent!
Any news about. . .	Oh I am pleased!
	How lovely!
	That's fantastic!
	Oh wonderful!
	Empathizing: (neutral)
	That's interesting.
	I know how you feel.
	That's quite an experience!
	Showing interest:
	Really?
	Goodness!
	How amazing / interesting!
	Never!
	Tough!
	Wow!
	That's serious.
	That's funny. . .
	Posing further questions:
	So what happens next?
	Will you. . .
	Are you going to. . .
	Have you decided. . .

1.9 I'm this type of person

Describing what you're like

Language focus   Adjectives to describe personality traits
                    Adverbs of degree

Level   Lower-intermediate upwards

Materials   Board, paper

Preparation   Review essential vocabulary

Procedure

FOR ADULTS AND TEENAGERS

1 Decide on the areas to be evaluated. (You can brainstorm names of
  qualities with the class – choose your own or select seven or so from
  Box 3.) Write them in a list down one side of the board, which
  learners copy.
2 Keep the list visible. Now draw a diagonal line across the board,
  which learners also copy. The ends of the line represent the two
  extremes. Each person, beginning with you, should now assess
  themselves on at least five of these by writing, at a point on the line
  that is true for them, a given personality factor. The result will
  obviously vary for each individual, but in an elementary class it might
  look like this:

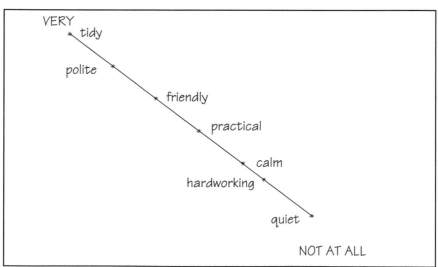

3 When everybody has completed their charts they should team up with a partner and discuss where they are on their line and where they would like to be. For example:

I'm not very quiet. I'd like to be a bit quieter.
I'm pretty tidy and that's how I want to be.

Variation for intermediate upwards

1 Ask the class to volunteer adjectives which they feel represent the stereotypical view of them as a nation.
2 In class or for homework, each learner then writes a short piece saying why they do/don't think they fit that stereotype.
3 When the writing is complete, learners form groups of three or four and discuss their self-assessment with each other.

Variation for small classes

With a class of around eight or fewer you can dispense with paper and pencil and use the room as a gauge.

1 Establish which end of the room represents VERY and which NOT AT ALL.
2 Starting with yourself, go to the point on the 'line' which you feel describes you in terms of, for example, how witty you are. Then ask learners to place themselves at a point on the line which describes where they think they fit on the line in terms of that same quality.
3 When everyone is in position, say where you are and where you would like to be – for example:

I'm not in the least bit witty, but I wish I were.

and walk to the point on the line where you would prefer to be. Learners then do the same, placing themselves in their ideal location for that particular quality.

Follow-on

a When you have done this for no more than five qualities, ask learners to individually rank the discussed qualities in order of desirability.
b Organize the class into two small groups and allow learners time to discuss their differing opinions.

FOR CHILDREN

Language focus Everyday activities

Follow the same pattern as for adults and teenagers, but substitute personality traits with things that children can assess themselves as being good or bad at, things they like or dislike, or even how frequently they do certain activities. There are ideas to choose from in Box 4.

Box 3 I'm this kind of person

Elementary adjectives

tidy, kind, calm, friendly, polite, practical, hardworking, quiet, helpful, funny

Intermediate adjectives

witty, energetic, generous, possessive, argumentative, bad-tempered, moody, honest, loyal, jolly, gentle, shallow, amusing, emotional, up-front

Advanced adjectives

uptight, critical, fiery, rational, conservative, thrifty, hedonistic, assertive, demanding, intense, reliable, trustworthy, consistent, unassuming, hidebound, diligent, vivacious, superficial, shrewd, avaricious

---

Box 4 I'm this kind of person

running, jumping, skipping, dancing, swimming, colouring, going shopping, washing up, walking, cooking, reading, knitting, making models, painting, drawing, sewing, watching TV, going to school, playing an instrument, going to the cinema, going to parties, playing games, listening to stories, going to friends' houses, dressing up, getting presents, visiting relatives, looking after other children

---

Acknowledgement

The idea of comparing yourself against a national stereotype comes from Bob Nessling.

1.10 How I feel about the language I'm learning

Giving reasons for your attitude to the target language

A follow-up version of this activity is used at the end of the course (Activity 8.8)

Language focus Stating how you feel and giving reasons

Level Lower-intermediate upwards

Materials Board

Procedure

FOR ADULTS, TEENAGERS AND CHILDREN

1 Ask learners to draw a series of four concentric circles to make their own personal 'linguagram'. Draw an example yourself on the board. In the centre circle they should write the name of the language they are learning. The circles then represent 'Very attractive', 'attractive', 'unattractive', and finally 'very unattractive'. They should indicate how they feel about the target language by marking an 'x' on the circle that most accurately describes their current attitude to the language they are learning.

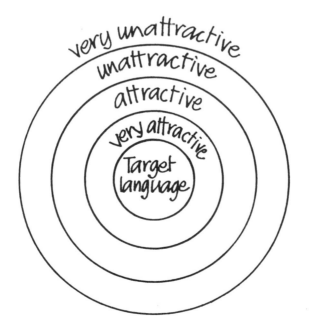

2 Now ask learners to do a walkabout activity in which the aim is to compare their feelings about, for example, English, with those of their classmates. They should use the exercise as an opportunity to say why they feel as they do. For example:

Ghada:	I really like English because I listen to a lot of English music and I love it.
Riita:	I don't like English much because I find the words very difficult to pronounce – I don't like the feel of English in my mouth!
Wolfgang:	I like English because it's the language I know best – I've learnt it for years and years!
Tuula:	I don't like English much because it's not a very pretty language but I have to learn it for my job – I can't do without it.

3 At the end of the activity, ask for volunteers to say whether they found anyone with similar attitudes to theirs.

Variation

Ask learners to draw their circles on a piece of paper that they can attach to themselves as a badge which they can wear during the walkabout at stage 2.

Note The badges can be kept and used again at the end of the course. See Activity 8.8.

2 Warming up

2.1 The personality you carry with you

Finding out what you have in common

Language focus   Relative clauses

Level   Lower-intermediate upwards

Materials   Each learner must have advance warning to bring with them three things, or, in the case of large items, drawings of things, which have been important to them in the last six months.

Preparation   Materials gathering

Procedure

FOR ADULTS AND TEENAGERS

1 Choose three items from your pocket or handbag which you feel say something about your personality, e.g. a photo of a relative, a donor card, a lottery ticket, a key ring with special significance.
2 Pair the students and ask them to write down three things which they can guess about the type of person the owner of the items (i.e. their teacher) is, beginning *The owner of these items is probably the kind of person* . . . Then ask them to read what they have written. For example:

> I think my teacher is the kind of person . . .
> − who is a bit sentimental
> − whose family is important to them
> − who thinks it's important to help people
> − who is optimistic
> − who thinks he/she might be lucky one day
> − who doesn't throw old things away

3 Now ask each learner to produce the three things which they have brought with them to class. In pairs, students look at each other's

objects or drawings and write down three things about their partner in the same form as before.

4 Pair the pairs so that there are now groups of four. In these small groups, each person reads out what they have written and their partner comments on how they feel about these observations.

Writing follow-on

a Learners work in groups of four. Each chooses one of their objects and writes what it is at the top of a clean sheet of paper.

b They pass their piece of paper to the person on their left. This person then has three minutes to write as many questions related to the object as possible. So for example, if someone had brought in a driving licence, some questions might be:

> How long have you had your licence?
> Do you like driving?
> Are you a good driver?
> Could you live your life without this licence?
> How long did it take you to get this document?

c At the end of the three minutes, the papers are again passed on to the person on the left, and more questions are added in three minutes. This happens once more, until the owner of the object is eventually presented with a questionnaire which they fill out and then use as the basis of a piece of writing about their object. For example, the text resulting from the above questions might run as follows:

> My driving test was one of the most important exams I ever passed. I took three tests before I passed. I don't like driving much but I rarely drive fast and I am safe. I have to have my driving licence as I need a car to take my son to school – there is no bus service.

d The third and fourth stages of the base activity could easily be adapted for learners to talk about a particular time in their lives, e.g. when they were ten years old. If objects were not available, photos could be brought, or even pictures drawn.

FOR CHILDREN

Children are usually more interested in talking about themselves than in finding out about other children. This adaptation provides young learners with a reason for finding out what is important to others.

1 Brainstorm a topic, e.g. 'animals', and ask learners to draw their favourite animal. Set a time limit!
2 Ask them also to write a few words about why they like this animal. For example *I like elephants because they use their trunks for washing themselves.*

" I like elephants because they use their trunks for washing themselves."

3 Place the drawings around the room and ask learners to see if anyone has chosen the same animal as they have and to find out if the reason is the same.

Variation

This exercise can be extended to asking children to work within other categories such as pets / family members / toys / places / rooms in their houses / activities. It lends itself very well to homework.

2.2 The parts of my life

Focusing on what is important in one's life

Language focus Likes and dislikes; giving reasons

Level Lower-intermediate upwards

Materials Board

Procedure

FOR ADULTS AND TEENAGERS

1 Ask learners to think for a minute of the good and bad things about their lives.
2 Draw this mental map on the board. It represents, broadly, the town or area the students live in. You will know the areas that are likely to interest your particular students so change and adapt as necessary.

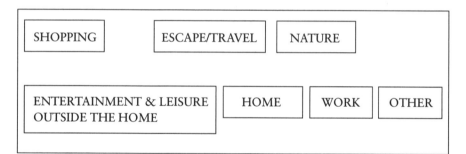

3 Tell learners that the classroom is divided into these seven areas. Ask them to go to a) the area they like most; b) the area they like second most; and c) the area they like least. When they reach each area they should find a partner and explain what they like about it and why. For example:

> I like home because I like everybody in my family! I feel very happy at home. I like having all my things around me. I can do what I like at home . . .

4 Tell the class that a magician has decided that they can choose one or two areas, but no more, in which to spend the next year of their lives. They must now choose which areas to 'live in' for a year. When they have chosen, they go and stand there. If they choose two, they simply move back and forth between them.

5 Allow them a minute to reflect, and then ask each learner to say something about the problems of living in their favourite areas. Here is part of an assessment of living in 'nature'.

> I chose 'nature' as one of my favourite places. There could be some problems living in 'nature' for a whole year! It would be difficult to escape from bad weather – you would probably have to build a shelter and that is hard work. Also in summer 'nature' can be quite a difficult place because . . .

FOR CHILDREN

Proceed as above, but use this map at stage 2.

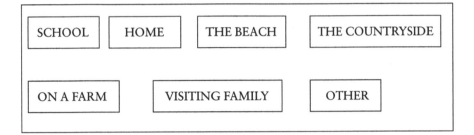

Writing follow-on

a Ask learners to think of two places they have lived, one which they liked and one they didn't. Write *good* and *bad* at the top of two columns on the board and then invite learners to brainstorm characteristics of each place.

b Now ask learners to make notes, using the headings below, about two places they have lived. If they have lived in the same place all their lives, ask them to choose another place they know well and to respond to as many of the headings as they can.

	Place one	Place two
Neighbours		
Friendship		
Type of area		
Look of the place		
Weather		
Standards of living		
Other		

This is how Kathy filled in part of her worksheet:

	Place one Simiad City	Place two Sidley Village
Type of area	City suburb	Rural
Look of the place	Cream and beige buildings, brown river, very little colour	Hills all around Very green – lots of rocky paths
Other	Tense; globally significant location	Busy, but not a very important place

c Then ask learners to use these notes to begin to write a contrastive text which includes information describing both places as well as their feelings towards them. There are typical 'compare and contrast' devices in Box 5. Below is part of Kathy's text:

> One of the things I didn't like about Simiad City was the colour of everything – it was only cream or beige. Sidley vllage is far more colourful than Simiad. It is in the hills and everything is green. The flowers in spring and summer are beautiful . . .
>
> Sidley is not an important place – it is just a little village. It is less than a tenth the size of Simiad, which is very famous. I think everybody knows about Simiad and has opinions about . . .

d Learners can finish off the text at home. The final phase of the class work should be to list the things that have made a place good or bad for them, from the most important to the least important, and display the results around the classroom.

Box 5 The parts of my life

but / although / however / on the one hand / on the other hand / while 1 is (adj). . . 2 is (adj). . . / the most / the least / twice as (adj). . . as / half as (adj). . . as / complete contrast to / more (adj) than / less (adj) than

---

2.3 Evaluating objects

Close observation

Language focus   Adjectives; giving reasons

Level   Elementary upwards

Materials   Copies of continua; board

Preparation   Review adjectives and prepare continua

Procedure

FOR ADULTS, TEENAGERS AND CHILDREN

1 Brainstorm 'objects you have been in contact with over the last twelve hours'. Make sure there is a really good mix of things on the board.
2 Tell learners they are going to classify some of the objects. Ask pairs to choose six things with which they have both been involved (not necessarily together) over the past twelve hours. Encourage learners to choose a variety of objects. A list such as TV, video, radio, etc. would be rather repetitive, whereas TV, pillow, and carpet, for example, would provide more variety. It is very important for the success of the activity that learners think of particular objects (e.g. **their** TV rather than TVs in general, **their** school bus rather than all buses) otherwise part 3 becomes impossibly difficult or even meaningless.
3 Give out the prepared continua. There are suggestions for three language levels in Box 6. Ask learners individually to classify each of their agreed six objects on these scales by writing its name at the appropriate point. When learners have completed this activity, they should compare their classifications with their partner's to see how closely their opinions match. If a scale is not appropriate for a particular object, students should leave it out. The following shows

how Kathy categorizes her computer, her house and her pillow, using three separate scales.

Example:

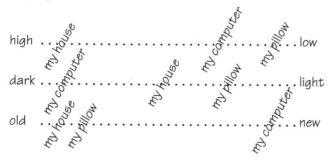

Variation for upper-intermediate

For upper-intermediate learners and above, give them examples of continua and ask them to develop five of their own.

Writing follow-on

Ask learners to choose one or two of the things they have been involved with over the past 12 hours (see preceding). Present them with the words from the continua for their level. Present also a range of adverbs appropriate to their level. (There are some suggestions in Box 7 at the end of this section.)

Ask them to write a short description of their thing without mentioning it by name, beginning with *My thing is* . . . They should leave some space around their text. Texts might look like this:

Elementary

i My thing is really new. It is soft but strong. It is quite colourful and it is nice to look at. It is for someone much younger than me.

Intermediate

ii My thing is made of plastic. Mine is modern, but you can get old-fashioned ones. It has teeth, but it doesn't bite. It is incredibly safe, in fact. It is extremely common. I never share mine with anyone and I use it at least once a day.

Advanced

iii My thing is made of plastic. It slots into a machine. When it works, it is marvellously efficient. I use it quite regularly and I'd be lost without it, though they didn't exist when I was a child. I suppose it is strong, yet I think of it as delicate and complicated as well. It is invaluable to me.

Note Answers to these can be found at the end of this chapter.

Display the texts around the room and invite all the learners to walk around, read what's been written and to hazard a written guess on the paper of what the 'thing' might be. Finally, ask the authors to write the name of their 'thing' as a heading to their text. Allow learners to walk around and check their guesses before closing the activity.

Box 6 Evaluating objects

Elementary continuum suggestions

high	low
dark	light
old	new
expensive	cheap
hard	soft
weak	strong
big	small
wide	narrow
boring	interesting
dirty	clean

Intermediate continuum suggestions

modern	old-fashioned
straight	curved
plain	patterned
huge	tiny
easy	complicated
ugly	attractive
safe	dangerous
vital	a luxury
delicate	strong
common	unusual

Advanced continuum suggestions

natural	artificial
rough	smooth
delicate	strong
intriguing	dull
appealing	revolting
complex	straightforward
well-designed	badly designed
useful	useless
scruffy	smart
efficient	inefficient
mild	harsh

Box 7 Evaluating objects

Elementary

a bit / quite / slightly / rather / somewhat / very / really

Intermediate

moderately / somewhat / definitely / terribly / extremely / incredibly / unbelievably / universally

Advanced

intensely / enormously / hugely / deceptively / desperately / unfailingly / intrinsically / decidedly / unquestionably / undoubtedly / vastly / worryingly

2.4 **Intensive pronunciation work**

Practice in problematic sounds

Language focus   Pronunciation of specific sounds
Level   Elementary upwards

Procedure

FOR ADULTS, TEENAGERS AND CHILDREN

1 Brainstorm 'Words that I find difficult to pronounce'. Write them on the board.
2 Ask learners to incorporate one or more of the words into a sentence about themselves, or one which is an expression of a personal opinion or belief.
3 Ask learners to pass their papers to the left and think of a new sentence which contains a word from stage 1 which they find difficult to pronounce. They should write it beneath the sentence already written.
4 Continue passing the papers round, with each learner writing a new problem pronunciation sentence on each neighbour's paper. If they run out of sentences, let them pass.
5 When the papers have reached their original owners, ask learners to read their new list of sentences individually, and to practise them quietly. Then ask them to rate each sentence on a scale:

   10 = extremely easy to pronounce
    0 = impossible to pronounce

6 Finish off with a round – *The easiest sentence for me to pronounce is . . .*

2.5 Careful listening

Describing sound

Language focus   Adjectives to describe sound
Level   Elementary and intermediate
Materials   Scale sheets
Preparation   Review adjectives to describe sound

Procedure

FOR ADULTS, TEENAGERS AND CHILDREN

1 Ask the class to relax, sit comfortably and close their eyes.
2 Ask them to listen hard for two minutes and count and remember all
   the sounds they hear.
3 When the two minutes have elapsed, ask them to write down the
   names of the sounds they heard.
4 Distribute prepared scales where learners should write in the names
   of the sounds they heard. Sounds may occur on more than one scale.
   For example:

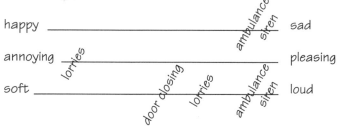

   There are scales for different levels shown in Box 8 at the end of this
   activity.
5 When learners have completed this stage individually, place them in
   small groups so that they can see what others have written.

For advanced learners

The activity proceeds in the same way as for elementary and intermediate learners, but instead of scales, they receive only one set of
words. They assess the sounds on a scale of, for example, very high-
pitched to not at all high-pitched, and then consider whether an
'opposite' can be found to write at the other end of the scale. Examples
can be found in Box 8.

Variation

If the sounds in and around your classroom are really limited, you could tape a selection of sounds (e.g. a car horn, a baby crying, a dog barking, a lullaby) and play them to the class to assess.

VARIATION FOR ADVANCED LEARNERS

This variation is particularly suitable if you have pre-recorded your own sounds.

Proceed in the same way as before, but provide learners with a set of words which are challenging for them to distinguish between. Examples of such words can be found in Box 8.

WRITING FOLLOW-ON

a Using the scales and ideas from the appropriate section of Box 8, ask learners to list a sound they know on each scale, in the place that seems right to them. Help with vocabulary, and suggest any extra adjectives for the advanced learners' scales as they are needed. One of Kathy's scales looks like this:

b Now ask them to choose one or two scales and to describe the sounds on it, including such information as:

- what time of day this is heard
- where you are when you hear this
- how often you hear this
- when you first and last heard the sound

Kathy's paragraph using the scale above reads like this:

> I hear the sound of the lorries rumbling past my house from four o'clock onwards every morning. I'm still in bed but obviously not in a deep sleep. About an hour later I hear my kids chatting to each other. The chatting usually turns to screams and the sound of monsters and sirens. Meanwhile, I am still in bed. These are my first alarm calls. If my husband is away, the next one is the phone – my husband checking to see that all is well.

c When learners have finished, you can choose for them to either

   i read out their paragraph

or

ii pin their paragraph up to be read by their classmates.

Box 8 Careful listening

Elementary scales

quiet	loud
high	low
nice	horrible
familiar	unfamiliar
scary	calming
relaxing	irritating

Intermediate scales

pleasant	unpleasant
frequent	infrequent
restful	noisy
distant	near
disturbing	comforting
alarming	soothing

Advanced words

high-pitched
distracting
soothing
shrill
enchanting
unrelenting
menacing
rhythmic
staccato
regular

Advanced variation

shrill / piercing / loud / noisy
quiet / soft / hushed / calm
annoying / irritating / disturbing / distracting
attractive / appealing / pleasing
regular / constant / frequent / unbroken

2.6 My world

Talking about where you live

Language focus   Places and prepositions of place

Level   Elementary upwards

Materials   Board

Preparation   Review prepositions of place

Procedure

FOR ADULTS, TEENAGERS AND CHILDREN

1 Establish, by a brainstorm if you don't already know, where the learners live.
2 In the centre of the classroom, indicate a central place which lies in the geographical centre of the learners' living area (or an important and fairly central local landmark).
3 Using this spot as a guide, and indicating the four points of the compass by pointing to the four walls of the classroom, ask learners to go to one of the places they like best in their area. Ask them to check their location by speaking to those around them.
4 Ask each learner to call out where they are and to say why they like this place. For example:

Stefan:	I'm in a bar called 'Film Dose'. I like it because it's really busy and lively!
Salem:	I'm in a café called 'La Strada'. I like it because I enjoy the pinball machines here.
Pauline:	I'm in the concert hall. I love to come here to listen to really beautiful music.
Eeva:	I'm in the market. I like to see the fresh fish and vegetables for sale.

5 Now continue, for as long as seems interesting, with other places they like, and perhaps a place they hate.
6 Finally, sketch a map on the board with all the places mentioned and the numbers of people who visited them.

WRITING FOLLOW-ON

a Ask learners to close their eyes and picture a favourite place. Then ask them to think about the place in the following categories:

sounds / colours / people / shapes / movement

b In class, or for homework, ask learners to write a paragraph about their place using the preceding topics. Emphasize above all that they shouldn't describe the place in any way that uses its name. A lower-intermediate text describing a church in use might look like this:

> In my place you can hear singing, chanting and people speaking the same words at the same time. The only bright colours are those of the robes and the windows. Most of the people who go to this place regularly are older than me. There are a lot of arches and people make the same movements at the same time.

c Here are two ways such texts can be used in class.

  i Display them so that they may be seen by everybody. Learners can be invited to walk around and read the texts. As they do so, they should write beneath as many of the texts as they can either the name of the place or the kind of place they think it is.
  ii Invite learners to read out their texts. Other members of the class try to guess what it is.

2.7 The best and the worst

Responding with feeling to news

Language focus   Expressing pleasure and sympathy

Level   Intermediate upwards

Materials   Slips of paper

Procedure

FOR ADULTS, TEENAGERS AND CHILDREN

1 On a clean piece of paper, with no names on it, ask learners to complete the following sentences:

The best thing that's happened to me this week is . . .
and *The worst thing that's happened to me this week is . . .*

Learners should write something that they are willing to share with the class and something that might be easily guessed by at least one other person in the class.

2 Collect and jumble the papers and carefully redistribute them so that everyone has somebody else's. Ask them to read out what they have, and then ask the class to suggest who they might belong to.

3 As this activity develops, elicit ways of expressing pleasure or sympathy, writing them on the board if necessary, and practising them as each contribution is read out. For example, if a learner has written

The worst thing that happened to me this week was that my haircut went badly wrong.

an appropriate guess might run

Oh dear. Is that your sentence Voitto? What a shame!

Suggested expressions can be found in the empathizing sections of Box 2, Activity 1.8.

4 To round off, invite learners to give their opinion as to who had the best thing happen to them.

Writing follow-on

a Brainstorm 'Disasters and awful things that can happen' followed by 'Wonderful things that can happen'.

b Now ask learners to write a dialogue between A and B. A describes either an awful or a wonderful event, while B responds totally inappropriately.

For example:

> A: I had an awful time last night . . .
> B: Really? How nice!
> A: Yes, to start with I lost my wallet in a car – I think it was stolen.
> B: Fantastic!
> A: Then my friends took me out to a restaurant and it was so late when I got home I was too tired to write my essay.
> B: Great!
> A: And then I was ill all through the night – I think it was the oysters.
> B: That's wonderful!

c In pairs, facing each other, learners now dramatically read their dialogues to the class. Allow time for rehearsal if necessary.

2.8 Making small talk

Social chit-chat

Language focus   Small talk

Level   Lower-intermediate upwards

Procedure

FOR ADULTS AND TEENAGERS

1 Ask the class to imagine that you are all at a party, wandering around with your drinks and making small talk. Each person should introduce themselves and ask each other *'How are you doing?' 'How's life treating you?'* etc. Emphasize that exchanges should last for no more than two to three minutes, then participants should excuse themselves with a typical phrase *'Well, it's been pleasant talking to you.'*
2 Continue the activity until it shows signs of running out of steam. This can vary, from our experiences, from five to forty minutes. The length of time you let it run also depends, of course, on the degree of free practice your class needs.

VARIATION

1 Brainstorm 'famous characters from history, films, books, politics', etc.
2 Ask each learner to choose a character they would like to portray and to think about them; about their character, mannerisms, the way they speak, and what they might talk about.
3 Invite learners to circulate in their new characters and talk to one another as described in the base activity. Adopt one of the characters yourself, and circulate with the learners.

....

Answers to 2.3 writing follow-on

  i a baby's teething ring
 ii a comb
iii a floppy disk

3 Acting, reacting, interacting

3.1 Reactions

Ascertaining how people feel

Language focus   Vocabulary of feelings

Level   Lower-intermediate upwards

Materials   Slips of paper with feelings on

Preparation   Organize slips of paper
Review vocabulary

Procedure

FOR ADULTS AND TEENAGERS

1 Divide the class into two groups, A and B. Tell learners they are going to work in pairs within their group. Give pairs in group A a slip of paper with one feeling written on it. There are ready-to-use ideas in Box 9.
2 Ask those in group A to represent the feeling using their whole body in the form of a live statue. They can move if they wish.
3 When group A learners are ready, group B learners should walk around looking at the live statues and trying to guess what feeling they represent. When everyone has had a chance to look at all the statues, a feedback session can follow, with group B learners saying what they thought were represented, by whom, and why. Discrepancies can be discussed and cultural differences in body language highlighted either between class members or between target culture and host culture.

Variation

Assign one feeling to pairs. One partner is the clay, the other the sculptor. The sculptors move the clay into the position they feel best represents the feeling. A viewing follows and then roles are exchanged.

Acknowledgement

We saw this variation at a workshop by Gavin Bolton.

Writing follow-on 1

Learners write a mini-dialogue which incorporates their assigned emotion. A dialogue for the feeling 'shock' might run as follows:

A: Have you heard the news?
B: No – what's happened?
A: The Prime Minister's been assassinated!
B: What?

Writing follow-on 2

a Learners choose five to ten of the feelings they have enacted.
b Give them this table, and ask them to complete it.

Name of feeling	Always welcome	Often welcome	Sometimes welcome	Rarely welcome	Never welcome

c When they have done this, ask them to choose one of the feelings and to write it at the top of a clean sheet of paper. Place these around the room (on walls or just on desks) and ask learners to walk around with a pencil ready. They should write a sentence which agrees or disagrees with the affirmation at the top of the paper, and should elaborate in some way. For example:

HUNGER IS NEVER WELCOME

But to know the feeling of hunger is a good thing. It can help us to remember that some people are always hungry and we can try to change that.

I'm not sure – knowing hunger means we think about what a bad thing it is to be hungry.

It isn't welcome if you have no food.

---

d When they have written a sentence on one paper, they should replace it, choose another and do the same again, and so on, until you stop them.

e After about ten minutes or so, when the papers are reasonably full, ask learners to collect their original papers and return to their seats.

f To round off, ask learners to share with the group anything now on their paper that they wouldn't have thought of themselves in connection with their 'feeling'.

Writing follow-on for advanced learners

a Proceed as for Writing follow-on 2 points a) and b). At point c), instead of responding simply to the main heading, ask learners to incorporate their responses to other learners' comments when they get to write their own. The same header sentence, although using a target word from the elementary set as the initial stimulus, could produce a writing sheet like this:

HUNGER IS NEVER WELCOME

But to know the feeling of hunger is a good thing. It reminds us that some people are always hungry and may make us try to rectify that.

Yes that's true. Personal experience of hunger can motivate us to do something for people who are always hungry.

It's true that personal experience of hunger can spur people on to help others. But I still think . . .

---

b Once the sheets are completed, proceed with points d) and e) as in Writing follow-on 2.

FOR CHILDREN

If you find that your young learners have difficulty working with decontextualized emotions, you may like to try this activity using the everyday situations provided in Box 9, or invent ones appropriate to your learners. Including more on the list than are being enacted makes it more challenging.

Box 9 Reactions

Elementary	Intermediate	Advanced
happiness	boredom	distress
sadness	puzzlement	alarm
fear	delight	ecstasy
cold	depression	disgust
tiredness	relaxation	relief
hunger	embarrassment	displeasure
thirst	worry	impatience
anger	helplessness	terror
surprise	dismay	annoyance

Young learner situations

Someone who is . . .

brushing their teeth   driving a car
washing their face   eating a lemon
combing their hair   making a cake
getting dressed   opening a present

51

eating breakfast	doing their homework
painting a picture	learning to play the piano
watching television	using a computer

3.2 Exact replication

Retelling, in a foreign language, what was told to you in that language

Language focus   Awareness of and practice in pronunciation

Level   Elementary upwards

Materials   A short story to read aloud or a taped story

Preparation   Pre-teach any unfamiliar vocabulary

Procedure

FOR ADULTS, TEENAGERS AND CHILDREN

1 Work with the whole class. The teacher tells or plays a very short story (no more than a minute long) once.
2 On the second hearing, stop after each sentence and ask different learners to repeat it exactly. Help them to try to be perfect.
3 Finally, learners hear the whole story again. When this is complete, ask for volunteers to retell it as it was originally told. Allow each volunteer to retell a different part of the story.

Follow-on

a When learners are familiar with this way of working, ask them to think of one incident that has recently happened to them; it could be something as small as meeting someone in the street. Here is one example of a short incident:

> On Tuesday morning I woke up at six o'clock. I was very tired. My little boy always wakes up early and he came to see me. I told him that I was very tired. He went away and I went back to sleep. At a quarter past six he came back to see me. He had brought me up 'breakfast' – a piece of bread with no butter – a chocolate biscuit and a children's yoghourt. He was very proud. He is only six years old, and so I was very proud too.

b Divide learners into pairs, As and Bs. As then have one minute (you need to time this) to tell Bs of the incident. B then tries to repeat it exactly, using the same words, the same intonation, etc. Then they exchange roles.

Writing follow-on for intermediate upwards

a Ask learners to recall another small recent incident and to write it in their mother tongue.
b In pairs, ask learners to dictate a translation of their story to a partner.
c The original mother tongue story is now read out to the whole class by its author in their own language, followed by the dictated translation, transferring the tone from the original.

3.3 Be my eyes

Communicating pictures in speech

Language focus   Detailed descriptions

Level   Upper-intermediate upwards

Materials   Pictures to display on the board

Procedure

FOR ADULTS, TEENAGERS AND CHILDREN

1 Ask the class to close their eyes. Tell them that you are going to describe a picture in detail.
2 Describe the picture as accurately as possible, using the kind of language you expect your learners will need when they come to do the task themselves, e.g. *in the top right hand corner, just to the left of this*, etc.
3 Place the picture you have described, along with some others, on the board. When you have finished describing the picture, ask learners to open their eyes and to identify which one you described.
4 Now pair learners and ask As to think of something they would like someone to describe. It might be one of the remaining pictures, or it could be something different – the view from the window, their own clothes, or their face, for example.
5 As then close their eyes and listen to Bs' descriptions. When this description has finished, learners exchange roles and A describes to B something that B would like described.

6 To round off the activity, ask learners what they had described to them. Write them up on the board.

Writing follow-on

a Ask learners to think of a person, place or thing that is special to them.
b Now ask them to write about her, him or it, using as many of the following headings as possible:

Size / Weight / Shape / Colour(s) / Touch / Smell / Taste / Sound

c Without identifying what is being described, or even whether it is person, place or thing, they write a description. They could begin *My special choice is . . .* (size) *and . . .* (weight) etc. For example:

> My special choice usually stands about half as tall as me and weighs around 35 kilos. The shape is hard to describe. It is a bit like a fairly large cylinder with five long thin cylinders and then something like a short cylinder attached to it. The colour is a beautiful deep gold. My thing is mainly soft to touch and its smell reminds me of farms. I wouldn't like to taste it! My special choice often sounds like a pig (though it isn't one).

At all costs, the identity of the special choice should be concealed!
d Pairs now exchange papers and read and guess what is being described. They write their guess at the bottom of the paper. The answer to the above description can be found at the end of this chapter.
e Display the work around the room. After everyone has studied it, the authors write the true identity next to the guess, and learners circulate again to read this.

Note The answer to the description in c can be found at the end of this chapter.

3.4 Creating a drama

Emotive exchanges

Language focus   Building emotive dialogues
Level   Lower-intermediate upwards
Materials   Board; slips of paper

Procedure

FOR ADULTS AND TEENAGERS

1 On the board, write up some utterances which could be included in a mini-drama, e.g.

   a *No, Mum, I'm not going to!*
   b *I think it's time I moved out!*
   c *I'm sorry, you've failed your test.*
   d *I'm afraid your son's behaviour is unacceptable.*

   There are more to choose from in Box 10 at the end of the activity.

2 Choose one and ask the class to think of some contexts in which these words might be said. For example, 'd' might be said by an angry parent, a strict school teacher, or one partner in a couple who disagree on child care.

3 Build up a mini-dialogue on the board with the class, choosing an agreed context. A dialogue based on 'd' for example, could develop as follows:

> *Context: Teacher complaining to a parent*
>
> Teacher: Can I have a word, please?
> Parent: Yes . . .
> Teacher: I'm afraid we had a problem with your son today.
>   He was playing where he's not supposed to, picked
>   some berries off the tree and then he rubbed them all
>   over another little boy's shirt! I'm afraid your son's
>   behaviour is unacceptable. Could you have a word
>   with him?.
> Parent: Well yes, but . . .

4 Now ask learners to think of something that has been said to them, or that they have said to someone else, that provoked a strong reaction. It could be recent or it could be something from a long time

ago. Ask them to write this down on a slip of paper. Help learners with the wording.

5 Collect the slips in and distribute one to each pair, making sure each pair receives someone else's 'line'. Tell them that the slips will be used in a future lesson. Ask the pairs to compose a mini-drama including the 'line' at some point and be ready to act it out. The drama should last about one to three minutes.

6 When everybody has finished, ask learners to enact the drama to the class. Other learners listen to see who has used their phrase.

7 At the end of the activity, invite learners to comment if they wish on how the mini-drama differed from the original context.

8 The remaining phrases can be used in a subsequent lesson.

Variation

If you feel that asking for something that has actually been said to your learners is too intrusive, you can ask them to think of something they would have liked to have either said themselves or to have had said to them that would have provoked a strong reaction. Examples are shown below:

If you're not happy with the way I am, just remember who brought me up!

I think you damage children and should leave teaching.

I don't think it's fair to stop me seeing my friends.

Why should you decide how I do my homework?

Box 10 Creating a drama – utterances

You're late again!

I think we should get divorced.

I'm sorry, you've failed your test.

Dad, I want to leave home.

Look – I wasn't here last night because I stayed at my boyfriend's/girlfriend's.

Mum – I don't want to stay on at school.

Don't park in my parking space!

I'm never going to speak to you again!

It's the same thing every morning – me shouting at you and you just taking your time over everything!

I'm afraid I just feel I can't live here any more.

You're not welcome in this house . . .

Will you just listen to me for once?

I know now that I was wrong. Can you forgive me?

More than anything else, I want to put things right.

If you don't tell me what you want, I can't do what you want!

How can I act like an adult when you treat me like a child?

3.5 Function review

Looking at language as functions

Language focus   Function practice
Level   Advanced
Materials   Board

Procedure

FOR ADULTS AND TEENAGERS

1 Brainstorm some language functions and write them on the board. There are lots of examples in Box 11 at the end of this activity.
2 Ask learners to think, individually, over the past week and to recall one or two functions that they have used in their own language. Ask them to think of exactly what they said and write it down. For example:

praising: *You're a really nice person!*
commiserating: *I'm sorry, you've failed your test.*

3 Make sure each learner has a piece of A4 size paper. Ask them to translate what they said into the target language and to write that down.
4 Now ask them to exchange papers with a partner. Their partner should write a response to what is on the paper. This is then returned to the original owner, who in turn writes their next response, and then passes it back to their partner who writes another response, and so on. The aim is to build up two dialogues per pair. For example:

Praising
A: You're a really nice person!
B: *Do you think so?*
A: Yes I do.
B: *Well, it's very kind of you to say so.*
A: I'd love to take you out some time . . .
B: *I have a very busy schedule . . .*
A: Well, so do I, but if you're free some time?
B: *I'll keep in touch.*
A: Do you have my number?
B: *I'm sure I have!*
A: I'll look forward to hearing from you.
B: *OK. Bye!*
A: Bye!

---

5 When the activity seems to be slowing down, ask learners to close the dialogues down.
6 Ask sample pairs to read at least one of their dialogues out.
7 Finally ask for volunteers to say what function they used and how the classroom dialogue compared to the real situation.
   For example:

I used the function of praising at the beginning of my dialogue. In real life, I said these words to a friend who is feeling very depressed. I wanted to help her feel better, and it is true that she really is a very nice person. The dialogue we wrote in class is very different, because it is about someone trying to turn down an offer of a date.

Variation

If you think your students would be uncomfortable giving examples out of their own life, this variation can be used.

1 Brainstorm 'language functions' and write them on the board. Ask pairs to choose one function and both to write it down as the first line of a dialogue. Allocate students roles as either A or B. Ask As to write a positive and helpful response to the initial comment and Bs a negative and unhelpful response. For example, two sample openings might be:

I'm sorry, but you're making far too much noise.
A: I know – the party's a bit out of control – I'll try to quieten them.

I'm sorry, but you're making far too much noise.
B: Yeah – it's our end of term party!

2 Now, exchanging papers for each line, pairs try to keep the dialogues going. This is easier if both become angry.

3 When dialogues are complete, ask pairs to read them out.

Box 11 Function review – functions with sample phrases

apologize:	I'm so sorry
congratulate:	Well done!
blame:	It's your fault.
thank:	Thank you so much.
express regret:	I'm so disappointed that . . .
raise objections:	That's all very well, but . . .
suggest:	Why don't we . . .
promise:	I'll definitely do that.
deny:	It wasn't me!
complain:	I'm afraid this just isn't good enough.
refuse:	I won't do it.
disapprove:	I'm afraid I don't approve of that.
persuade:	Go on – just have a look at least.
explain:	This is what you do . . .
agree:	Absolutely!
threaten:	If you don't help me, I'll never speak to you again.
express hope:	I feel very optimistic.
give permission:	Yes, you can go out tonight.
consent:	All right, I'll try to help.
express hope:	Let's hope so.
show concern:	Is everything OK?
give advice:	Perhaps you ought to be doing something about it.
make an excuse:	Friday's no good – we're going away.
lie:	I'm a millionaire actually.
praise:	Well done!
show uncertainty:	I'm not quite sure about that.

3.6 Telling lies

Discerning the truth

Language focus Multi-form practice
Level Lower-intermediate upwards

Procedure

FOR ADULTS, TEENAGERS AND CHILDREN

1 Tell the class you are going to speak to them for a minute about yourself. In that minute you will include some information that is true and five things that are not. Their task is to work out from your manner, or their existing knowledge of you, what is not true.
2 When you have completed your speech, and learners have guessed, group them into sets of four.
3 Tell learners that they will now, in turn, address their small group, each talking for a minute and telling some truth and three lies each. Learners may make notes. After everyone has spoken, the members of the small group decide together what is not true for each individual.

Variation

1 Learners construct a written history of themselves which incorporates, say, four falsehoods. Place these where they can be seen by everybody.
2 Ask learners to walk around the class trying to spot what is not true. They can indicate this on the paper.
3 After a pre-agreed time limit, ask learners to indicate on their own papers what is not true.
4 Allow a few more minutes for them to check whether or not their hunches were right.

Acknowledgement

We first encountered the idea of telling lies in activities at a workshop by Christine Frank.

3.7 Language challenge

Specific language revision

Language focus   Revision of specific vocabulary
Level   Intermediate upwards
Materials   Board

Procedure

FOR ADULTS AND TEENAGERS

1 On the board, brainstorm the areas of vocabulary you have covered. For a lower-intermediate class these might include, amongst others:

   clothes / kitchen equipment / geographical features / parts of the body / shops and buildings

2 Choose an area yourself and speak to the class for 20 seconds. You may choose to review, for example, the vocabulary area of 'kitchen equipment' by describing your own kitchen to the class. For example:

> My kitchen is quite small. It hasn't got enough cupboards, so my saucepans live on top of the high cupboards, which is a nuisance. I cook a lot. I have eight saucepans – four with black handles that I bought myself and four aluminium ones with red handles that my mother gave me. I really like them. I can remember them from my childhood. I have a washing machine that is quite reliable – it's only flooded once – and a small dishwasher which I really like. I don't have a microwave as I absolutely hate them. I have a toaster which I am soon going to teach my children how to use so that they can make me my breakfast!

3 At the end of the monologue, ask learners to compare with a partner how much they can remember of what was said. Below is part of a dialogue between two learners remembering a teacher's kitchen description:

> Matti: She said she had eight saucepans.
> Arja: Yes – four with black handles and four with red handles that her mother gave her . . .
> Matti: They are made of aluminium . . .
> Arja: Yes, and she has a dishwasher – a small one.

> Matti: But no microwave!
> Arja: No! But she has an old washing machine that has flooded
>   once.

4 Now, in the same pairs, ask learners to choose one of the language
   areas they would like to speak on. When the pair has agreed, tell
   them that they are each going to have to speak on the area for 30
   seconds. Give them some time to plan and make notes of what they
   are going to say individually.
5 When everyone is ready, ask one pair to sit in the middle of the class
   circle. One learner then speaks to the other for 30 seconds. Roles are
   then reversed. At the end of the 60 seconds, the pair return to their
   seats and another pair take their turn in front of the class and so on
   until everyone has spoken.

Variation

With advanced-level classes, this activity can be turned into a competition and the language aim extended to cover all types of language
revision, with pairs vying to be the best at whatever particular language
area they are practising. Examples could include:

- poetic images – each contestant describes a beautiful scene they love
- love – each contestant speaks of love
- interruptions – each contestant speaks while the other tries to butt in
  with appropriate interruptions
- talking at the same time – each contestant keeps up a stream of talk at
  the same time as their partner.

Pairs speak in front of the class, as with the main activity. After each
pair has spoken, the class votes to decide on the winner.

Writing follow-on

Vocabulary revision

a Tell learners they will practise detailed descriptions. Ask them to
   think of a place or object that is special to them. Ask what the places
   or things are, and then make sure learners narrow down the size and
   complexity of their chosen thing or object by thinking of an aspect of
   it. For example, a favourite room should be reduced to one object in
   it (a chair, vase, carpet, etc.); a landscape to a tree, bridge or rock,
   etc.
b Now, giving learners a set amount of time, ask them to describe their
   object in the minutest detail, including all of the following if relevant.

- exact size
- age
- materials
- how and by who manufactured
- colour / pattern
- smell / shape / texture
- how useful / beautiful / valuable
- who likes it, who sees it and how often
- history in the future

For example:

> My object is small – I can hold it in my hand. It is eight years old
> and not heavy at all. It was carved in Finland and so it is different
> shades of brown all over because the light shines differently on
> each part. It used to smell of wood, but it doesn't smell of
> anything now. It is the shape of a brown bear looking down and
> it is not smooth, because of the carving. It is meaningful to me
> because it reminds me of Finland and useful because I give it to
> my little daughter to hold when I comb her hair to stop her
> crying. I don't think it is valuable. My children love it and look
> at it every day, and so do I. I think my children will keep it and
> show it to their children – it will become an heirloom!

c When complete, let the 'object biographies' be displayed on the walls
for class reading.

3.8 Congratulations

Congratulating each other

Language focus   Congratulating
Level   Lower-intermediate upwards
Materials   Sticky labels; board

Procedure

FOR ADULTS, TEENAGERS AND CHILDREN

1 Ask learners to think of the nicest thing that has happened to them
recently. Then ask them to write it on a sticky label or piece of paper.

2 Brainstorm many ways of congratulating people and expressing pleasure. Add your own if the list is too sparse.

3 Ask learners to display their happy event by sticking or pinning it on themselves. Then circulate, shaking hands and expressing their pleasure at each other's good fortune until all have congratulated and been congratulated.

4 The following are some examples of language you might expect to hear:

Brilliant! I'm really pleased you've got a part in the school play.

Well done – I'm delighted to hear you drove on the motorway for the first time.

Congratulations. I'm so happy your rabbit is well again.

Fantastic! It's so nice to know you won a prize at the weekend.

Writing follow-on

a Pair learners. Ask them to think of a recent personal achievement. The activity works best if learners choose something very simple, such as 'I managed not to mislay my glasses all week.' They should write this down and give it to their partner.

b Now suggest they write a short message congratulating their partner on this achievement. The should be as complimentary as possible. For example:

Dear Zuhair

I was so pleased to hear that you managed not to mislay your glasses all week. It's so easy to just put them down and forget about them, but you didn't do that! You should be really proud of yourself for managing to find them whenever you wanted them. Well done indeed!

Best wishes

Hanna

---

c Finally, learners give their written congratulations to their partners.

....

Answer to 3.3 Writing follow-on

My Labrador dog

4 Self-awareness and self-assertion

4.1 Stop the stranger talking

Strategies for avoiding conversation

Language focus   Polite responses; initiating and avoiding conversation
Level   Upper-intermediate upwards
Materials   Set of situations
Preparation   Organize slips

Procedure

FOR ADULTS

1 Set the chairs out in the pattern of seats on a bus. Divide the learners into two groups, A and B. 'A' people are very talkative, and 'B' people are polite people who are less talkative.
2 Now allocate roles. Bs all have the same role – a polite, untalkative person going home by bus. As are all people who want to start a conversation. Learners can choose from the role suggestions in Box 12. Allow each pair to look at A's role and give them some time to think of what might be said after A's first line.
3 After preparation time, sit As in chairs and ask Bs to board the bus and sit next to As. Essentially, As try to initiate a conversation and Bs respond in a polite way whilst trying to block or limit their involvement (a common situation in casual dialogue).
4 After three minutes, Bs rise, walk to the front of the bus and say 'Next stop, please.'
5 Elicit from the class the ways that Bs held back from fully entering the conversation. Some specific phrases will emerge, e.g. *'Oh really?'* *'I'm sorry to hear that'*, *'What a shame'*. Just as important as isolating these is to highlight the significance of minimal facial expression, muted body language and an uninterested intonation pattern in situations where you do not wish to be forced into conversation.
6 In some classes you may wish to give learners the opportunity to describe how they felt, how polite or impolite they thought they were, how they tried to keep conversations going and so on.

Extract from a sample conversation

A: Is this the bus to Manchester?
B: Yes, it is.
A: Oh, thank goodness for that – I'm never sure which one it is.
B: (Weak smile)
A: It's so difficult now that they've knocked down the bus
     station . . . I never know which stop to go to . . .
B: (Mmm)
A: I'm going for an interview, you see, so I wouldn't want to be
     late!
B: No.
A: Where is the bus? Is it always so late?
B: I really don't know.

Follow-on

Look at the phrases that were used to avoid involved conversations.
Show how these same phrases can be used to continue conversations by
using welcoming body language, lively facial expression, and intonation
patterns to show interest.

Box 12 Stop the stranger talking

Situations with suggested first-liners

Person worried about whether they're on the right bus.
Is this the bus to. . .?

Unwell person
Ooh, I do feel ill!

Aggressive person
Do you need the whole seat?

Person anxious not to miss their stop
Is this the eye hospital?

Person wanting to talk about a trip abroad
I've just come back from. . . the weather's quite different there.

Someone annoyed about the lateness of the bus
Is this bus always so unreliable?

Someone finding it difficult to get comfy
I'm sorry – these seats really aren't big enough for two people!

Someone who's just bought a new bike
I won't have to use the bus for much longer – I'm going to be cycling everywhere!

Football fan
I don't suppose you know who won the match today?

4.2 Survival

Persuasion techniques

Language focus   Persuading; names of professions

Level   Intermediate upwards

Materials   Slips of paper

Preparation   Review the language of persuasion

Procedure

FOR ADULTS AND TEENAGERS

1 Brainstorm all the occupations the class can think of. When the class has run out of ideas, add any you would like to see (unpaid jobs like 'housewife' for instance).
2 Ask learners to choose the two jobs they would most like to do in order of preference and to note them down. Split the class into groups of eight to ten and ask them to check that each person has chosen a different job. If their first choice has gone, the second will have to be used.
3 Tell each group that they are marooned on a desert island. Food and water are dwindling. The groups have already decided that half of the members must try to reach another island on a raft. This is extremely dangerous and everyone very much wants to stay where they are.
4 Grouped round a table or in a circle, each group member tries to persuade the others, in a timed two-minute speech, why he or she should be allowed to stay by stressing the skills and qualities a person with the job they chose in stage 2 brings to the situation. Give the learners a few minutes to prepare their speeches. Stress that decisions should be reached solely on the strength of the arguments. After each

speech, each group member writes the name of the speaker, followed by *stay* or *go*, on a clean piece of paper.

5 After all the speeches have been heard, each group should run its own final vote – the teacher doesn't have to know the result. Then announce that everyone has been saved by a friendly fishing boat!

Variation 1

Brainstorm hobbies instead of jobs.

Variation 2

Make the activity more challenging by asking learners to choose the jobs they would least like to do.

Follow-on

a Brainstorm 'adjectives that describe personal qualities' (*intelligent, sympathetic, tough, hardworking, pleasure-loving, selfish, lazy*, etc.)

b Now ask learners to choose the five that describe them best and the five that least describe them. They should write them in a column on the right-hand side of a piece of paper, the best first and the least last.

c Now ask them to choose five which are desirable in the job they would like to do. (They can include any they think are important that aren't on the list.) They should write them, in order of importance, on the left-hand side of the paper opposite the five qualities they have already written.

d Now ask learners to write a paragraph convincing their partner of how well they are suited to their ideal job.

e Display their mini-essay and their list of qualities around the room.

SAMPLE TEXTS

Teacher		
Ideal qualities	*My personality*	*Not me at all*
organized	kind	cold
efficient	quick to anger	rude
hard-working	understanding	lazy
fair	industrious	disorganized
approachable	critical	tough

I think I am exactly the right sort of person to be a teacher. In my opinion, it is very important for a teacher to be understanding. A kind, understanding teacher makes learners feel comfortable, so my students would certainly feel comfortable with me. As an industrious person, I would make my lessons interesting and homework would always be individually marked. On the negative side, I can be quick to anger, but I don't show it, so my learners wouldn't be aware of this, and my temper dies down very quickly too. It's true that I am rather critical, but this is balanced out by being understanding. In some ways, a critical approach could be helpful; I would be looking for learners to achieve their best.

4.3 Empathizing and persuading

Defusing anger with calm

Language focus   Persuasion

Level   Upper-intermediate upwards

Preparation   Review the language of persuasion

Procedure

FOR ADULTS AND TEENAGERS

1 Invite learners to brainstorm the most recent situations they re-member where they have felt really angry. Then ask them to shout out words and phrases that they used, or could have used.
2 Explain the significance of fist-clenching, and tell learners they are going to use friendly, helpful language to reduce extreme anger.
3 Recalling the situation in which they were last really angry, As clench their fists and explain their anger to Bs, who try to get As to be less angry, trying at the same time to empathize with As' anger. After four minutes, the roles are exchanged. The angry people unclench their fists only if they really feel persuaded by their partner of the importance of being less angry.
4 End with a round *During that activity I felt . . . while being the angry person and . . . while being the calming person.*
For example:

   I felt uncomfortable being the angry person and superior being the calming person.

70

I felt determined being the angry person and nervous being the calming person.

Writing follow-on

a Explain that you are going to suggest an activity which may help to rid learners of any remaining feelings of anger. Ask them to think of someone, or something, they really love, that makes them feel happy.
b Now ask learners to write for ten minutes, as fast as they can, and without correction or concern for grammatical perfection, starting with the words *What I really love about . . .* with as many examples from real life as they can.
c Stop the writing when the activity seems to be running out of steam.
d Finally tell learners that they can display their writing round the room for others to see if they wish. Encourage them to personalize the pieces pictorially in some way – for example, a border round the writing, or a corner illustration related to the text in some way.

What I really love about Bria is how much fun she is. She is three years old and has a wonderful sense of humour. I like the way she skips everywhere instead of walking. I love her interest in science-fiction toys. She can build her own small spaceships out of blocks. I like her unusual ideas about how to wear clothes – like tying her socks around her feet in bows. I like the way she tells me that our dog has 'spoken' to her (she always knows exactly what he has said). I love all these things and many more about Bria.

What I really love about Bria is how much fun she is. She is three years old and has a wonderful sense of humour. I like the way she skips everywhere instead of walking. I love her interest in science fiction toys. She can build her own small spaceships out of blocks. I like her unusual ideas about how to wear clothes – like tying her socks around her feet in bows. I like the way she tells me that our dog has "spoken" to her (she always knows exactly what he has said). I love all these things and many more about Bria.

4.4 Making people laugh

Trying to change someone's mood with words

Language focus   Cajoling
Level   Intermediate upwards

Procedure

FOR ADULTS, TEENAGERS AND CHILDREN

1 Divide learners into As and Bs. As are intensely serious and have vowed never to laugh or smile again. Bs are jovial characters.
2 Facing each other, Bs try to make As laugh as many times as they can by using mainly verbal means, though grins and gestures are permitted. Ways could include, for example, singing a song, telling a joke, reciting a nonsense rhyme, using a silly voice. Emphasize that As should only laugh if they really want to.
3 After two minutes, stop the activity and get feedback on how many times each B got A to laugh: four times? Once? Not at all?
4 Exchange roles.
5 At the end of the activity, find out what made who laugh. If it feels appropriate, ask the B role person within that pair to share what they said to their A partner with the rest of the class.

Writing follow-on

a Pair learners with new partners. Ask them individually to think of the funniest joke they know. Ask them now to write down the joke, omitting the last line, or punch line.
b Now ask learners to exchange papers, and try to guess the missing line.
c Papers are now returned to their authors. As with the base activity, one partner adopts a grim, unsmiling expression, while the other reads the joke with the original punch line and thus tries to make their partner smile against their will. In small classes, pairs may do this in turn, listened to by the whole class.

4.5 I'm like that too

Building up rapport in class

Language focus   Personal descriptions; adjectives of personal description

Level   Intermediate upwards

Materials   Board

Procedure

FOR ADULTS, TEENAGERS AND CHILDREN

1 Brainstorm words that describe people in terms of personality and interests as well as physical characteristics.
2 Learners and the teacher then write something about themselves using three to five such words, e.g.

I'm Chad. I'm fairly short, with very dark eyes. I'm strong-willed and observant, and I'm very interested in model trains.

Help learners with these short descriptions where needed, as stage 5 uses them again.
3 The teacher first reads out their description of themselves. After each key word, the teacher pauses and looks around the class. Anyone who feels a kinship calls out *I'm like that too* and notes down the teacher's name and the shared characteristic.
4 When the teacher has finished, divide the class into groups of eight to ten. Ask for a volunteer from each group to read out their description, again pausing after each key word for learners within their group to claim kinship and to note down the learner's name and similarity. Continue, allowing everyone a turn.
5 After the round is completed, ask learners to write a description of themselves which incorporates all the similarities to fellow-learners that they noted.

Writing follow-on for a class with penfriends

Ask the penfriends to write a self-description of specified length. Display them round the room. Ask learners to read them and to note down phrases that they could apply to themselves. They should then incorporate these into a written self-description.

4.6 What can be asked?

Gauging appropriacy

Language focus   Appropriacy and question practice
Level   Intermediate upwards
Materials   Board and questionnaires
Preparation   Copying or preparing lists

Procedure

FOR ADULTS

1 On the board, write these three questions:

What's your name?
How old are you?
Where do you live?

2 Ask learners if they would feel comfortable hearing a teacher ask these questions of them and their peers in class. They don't need to answer – just to consider. Explain that, in the reverse situation in Britain, it would be considered generally inappropriate for a learner to ask a teacher their age.
3 Give learners Questionnaire 1 from Box 13 at the end of this activity. Ask them to go through individually, deciding which questions they consider would make people feel uncomfortable if asked by their teacher publicly in class.
4 When they have finished, ask them to compare their decisions in groups of four and to agree a set of questions from the list that they as a group consider unacceptable.
5 Now jigsaw the groups. Ask them to look at the same list again and to decide which questions they would personally consider it inappropriate to be asked in private by a fellow learner.
6 Finally, ask groups to add two more unacceptable questions to their lists.

Follow-on

For homework, ask learners to think of appropriate situations for any of the questions they decided on as unacceptable.

Variation

Use the far more controversial Questionnaire 2 for a more 'issues'-based lesson.

Writing follow-on

Ask learners to write a questionnaire entitled *Questions not to ask strangers*. Specify a minimum number of questions, and suggest they incorporate any they have personally experienced if they wish. *Depending on your class, you may be able to use these in 4.7.*

Box 13 What can you ask?

Questionnaire 1

Part 1   **Personal information**

   1   What's your middle name?

   2   How old are you?

   3   How tall are you?

   4   How much do you weigh?

   5   Are you married? / Have you got a boy/girlfriend?

Part 2   **Target language – past and present**

   6   Are you enjoying your course?

   7   Do you work on the language you are learning after class?

   8   When did you first start learning this language?

   9   Do you like this language?

  10   Do you like your language teacher?

Part 3   **Financial information**

  11   How much money do you earn?

  12   How much money have you got in the bank?

  13   Have you got any savings?

  14   Are you ever overdrawn at the bank?

  15   Do you owe any money?

Part 4   **Status symbols**

  16   How old is your car?

  17   How much did you pay for it?

  18   What sort of neighbourhood do you live in?

  19   What is your house worth?

  20   Where do you shop for clothes?

© Cambridge University Press

Questionnaire 2

  1   What do you think of this country's leader?

  2   Do you consider yourself left- or right-wing?

  3   Should women have the vote?

  4   Do you think there are too many immigrants in this country?

  5   Do you think military service is a good thing?

  6   Do you believe in war?

  7   Do you believe in God?

  8   Are you religious?

  9   What are your feelings about euthanasia?

10   How do you feel about divorce?

11   Do you think couples should be married if they want to live together?

12   Do you think drugs should be decriminalized?

13   Have you ever taken drugs?

14   Do close friends of yours take drugs?

15   Do you believe in the death penalty?

16   Do you ever exceed the speed limit?

17   Have you ever smacked a child?

18   Do you believe in physical punishment?

19   Do you think teachers have the right to hit pupils?

20   Do you think prisons do any good?

© Cambridge University Press

4.7 Deflecting questions

How to not answer questions

This activity can be used as a follow-on to 4.6.

....

Language focus   Avoidance techniques

Level   Upper-intermediate upwards

Materials   Sticky labels or paper and pins

Preparation   Review deflection techniques

....

Procedure

FOR ADULTS AND TEENAGERS

1 Give learners parts 1, 3 and 4 of Questionnaire 1 from Activity 4.6.
Give them time to look through and to identify two questions which
they would not like to be asked on meeting someone for the first time.

2 On the board, write the question *How old are you?* Ask learners to think of polite responses to this question which avoid answering it. Write these up. Examples may include:

Partial answers

I'm in my thirties / forties.
I'm under 40.
I'm over 50.

Jocular answers

Over 21.
Old enough to drink!
Old enough to drive!

Firm but friendly refusals to answer

Old enough to know you shouldn't be asking that.
Old enough to tell you not to ask me that again.
Old enough to know it's bad manners to ask that question.

Confrontational answers

I really don't think you should ask me that.
Do you make a habit of asking inappropriate questions when you meet people?
I think that's my business, don't you?

---

3 Now, working in groups, learners choose one or two questions from each category and work out deflecting answers. Help them as they do this and make sure all questions are covered by the class as a whole.

4 Now ask all the learners to pin one of the questions they've worked on to themselves. A walkabout activity follows. Learners are asked their question by other members of the class. They can try out the different answers they have thought out as different people ask them their question.

5 To round off, line learners up around the room and ask them their question. They can deflect in the way they decided was most comfortable for them during the walkabout.

Variation

Instead of using the prepared questionnaires, you may like to use the questions learners prepared in the writing task in 4.6.

Follow-on 1

Learners create a contextualized dialogue with a partner which incorporates one question from each section of Questionnaire 1.

Follow-on 2

Learners select a question from Questionnaire 1 in 4.6. They then write three to four sentences in reply, but make them so vague that it's not immediately obvious which question each is answering. They then pin the pieces of paper to them and circulate, with their classmates reading the sentences and trying to guess the question.

4.8 Being sympatheric

Supporting in positive and negative situations

Language focus   Expressions of sympathy and support

Level   Intermediate upwards

Materials   Board

Preparation   Practise phrases from initial brainstorm

Procedure

FOR ADULTS AND TEENAGERS

1 Brainstorm 'how to sympathize'. Give learners some examples, if necessary, and add your own at the end to achieve as rich a supply as possible. Encourage both verbal expressions (e.g. *What a shame!*) and things you might do (e.g. put your arm round him/her). Some examples of verbal expressions can be found in Box 14.
2 Divide learners into pairs. A and B choose contrastive roles. A should think of something they have done at which they have been successful and B should think of something they have done which has been less successful than they would have liked. The point is for both to show support for each other, though this will probably be easier for the 'winner'. Below is part of an example dialogue.

> A: Hi Kaarina. How are you?
> B: Oh really well. I've just passed my driving test.
> A: Congratulations. You must be very pleased.
> B: Yes, I am. You don't look too happy though?
> A: No. I think I'm going to have to repeat year 10.
> B: Really? I'm amazed!
> A: So am I!
> B: Well – it's not the end of the world. I'm sure you'll do really well next time.

3 At the end of the activity, elicit all the new phrases that emerged, including such typical ones as *It's not the end of the world.*

Variation

If you feel your class would be too self-conscious using real-life situations, you can either

a ask them to invent their own situations;
b ask them to think back to a time in the past where they did/didn't succeed at something;
c use the situations from Box 15.

Box 14 Being sympathetic – Language expressing support

In positive situations	**In negative situations**
That's good news!	How awful!
Well done!	Sorry to hear that!
You've done very well!	What a shame!
What an achievement!	How disappointing!
That's excellent!	Well, you can always try again.
You must be very pleased.	Well, these things happen.
That's really good.	How unfortunate!
Brilliant!	Oh no!
Fantastic!	That's a shame.
Great!	How annoying!

Box 15 Being sympathetic

A roles	**B roles**
passed an exam	failed an exam
finished a difficult piece of work	haven't had time to finish off the work
got the CD he/she wanted for. . .	was given the wrong CD for. . .
parents helping with. . .	parents being very difficult
lost weight on a diet	haven't lost weight despite the diet
got a pay rise	didn't get a bonus
got a company car	car allowance being taken away
got tickets to a concert	tickets to concert sold out
received a nice letter from. . .	haven't heard from. . .
had an unexpected phone call	didn't get any phone calls from. . .
saw a really interesting film	had a boring night in
didn't need any work done at the dentist	had three big fillings at the dentist

---

4.9 Being assertive

Establishing an assertive manner

....

Language focus   Assertiveness

Level   Upper-intermediate upwards

....

Procedure

FOR ADULTS AND TEENAGERS

1 Divide the board into three and write *assertive, unassertive*, and *aggressive* at the top of each column. Then brainstorm words which are suggested by each of these three types of behaviour. These should include tone of voice, level of eye contact, and posture.

2 In pairs, ask learners to discuss which of these three groups they belong to and to think of a situation where they might be unassertive or aggressive.

3 Model three ways of dealing with a familiar situation. One which works well is teenage responsibility for housework within the family. Three approaches to the teenager are outlined below:

> **Unasssertive**
>
> Listen – I'm finding the housework too much for me on my own.
> I know you've got lots to do, but do you think that maybe, just
> now and again, you could help me a bit? All this housework
> makes me so tired!
>
> **Aggressive**
>
> You're always doing nothing. I'm fed up of your laziness. If you
> don't do the dishes you'll get a slap. Do you hear me?
>
> **Assertive**
>
> I'd really like some help tonight with the dishes . . . now I know
> you have a lot to do, but so have I. I need the help and I'd
> appreciate it now.

4 The important thing to communicate is that assertiveness entails

  a politeness and a respect for others' rights;
  b a reasonable insistence that your own rights and feelings must be
    kept in balance with theirs.

Both threats and self-pity must be avoided.

5 In pairs, learners develop mini-dramas, preferably based on real
situations they have experienced. They outline the situation and then
attempt to tackle the person most concerned using the assertive
language.

Follow-on

a Learners choose a situation; brainstorm, or provide a list:

- returning a faulty camera
- asking for an extension on an essay
- objecting to a parking ticket a traffic warden has just given
- complaining about the quality of a meal in a restaurant
- asking a large, tough-looking man to stop smoking in a non-
  smoking area
- asking some drunken students next door to keep the noise down
- refusing to lend someone some money
- complaining to your teacher about your lack of progress

b Learners choose a scenario. They then write a short dialogue between
themselves and the other person in the scenario, written in either
unassertive (U), assertive (A), or aggressive (AG) mode.
c Display the dialogues at the end of the activity.

5 Values and values awareness

5.1 Valued possessions

Value awareness

Language focus   Conditional clauses
Level   Upper-elementary upwards
Materials   Clean sheets of paper; music (optional)

Procedure

FOR ADULTS, TEENAGERS AND CHILDREN

1 Write the word *home* on the board. Then ask the class, with eyes closed if they wish, to think of the place they think of as home and to think of the most precious things in it. You may wish to provide some background music while they are thinking.
2 Tell them that there has been a fire, and that, while all the people and pets are perfectly safe, the house is blazing beyond control. The fireman yells down from the ladder that he can save four things only. Learners must decide (individually) which four things should be saved from their home. Two examples from different classes can be seen below.

> Alexander: I'd save my toy police-station, my train-set, my walking boots and my car-crusher.
> Yvette: I'd save my sister's jewellery box, the photos of the children as babies, my back-up computer discs and my handbag.

3 On a clean piece of paper, ask them to write down the names of the items they have decided to save, and their approximate monetary value.
4 Display the sheets of paper round the walls for all to see.

5 Lead a round *If I could save only one thing it would be . . . because
. . .* For example:

> | Yvette: | If I could save only one thing it would be my back-up computer discs because I'm doing a lot of work on a project at the moment – it's taken years! (And my mother has some photos of the children as babies!) |

6 In classes where the activity has been well received, learners can reclaim their sheet of paper from the wall and discuss in small groups the whys and wherefores of what they would save. It is likely to lead on to a discussion on personal values.

Acknowledgement

An activity similar to this appears in *Caring and Sharing in the Foreign Language Class* by Gertrude Moskowitz.

5.2 Mock auction

Describing things positively

Language focus   Persuading through positive description

Level   Lower-intermediate upwards

Materials   Paper and mock money

Preparation   To have completed 5.1 as a class

Procedure

FOR ADULTS AND TEENAGERS

1 This activity could well be timed to follow 5.1. Learners are told that they are left with only one object or possession, but that they may choose what it is. They then write its name on a slip of paper.
2 Jumble the slips and redistribute them. Now ask the learners to make a list of the qualities of their object – its desirability, usefulness and aesthetic value, for example.
3 Either give each learner a set of ten pretend notes of a fairly high value (£50 notes if the target language is English), or ask them to make their own using a clean sheet of paper, dividing it into ten rectangles and writing the agreed value on each.

4 Each person then auctions their new object. They should try to get as high a price as possible. You may need to model an auction and explain competitive bidding. Learners should understand that they need to preface each sale with inflated comments, using the lists made at stage two as prompts. They will also need to urge buyers if bidding is slow or flagging.

For example:

COME ON NOW LADIES & GENTLEMEN ..
THIS BAG IS MADE OF THE BEST GRADE
LEATHER. YOU CAN SEE HOW SOFT IT IS
AND IT REALLY IS CHIC! DO I HEAR £150 ?

CARVERS
AUCTIONEERS

5 After the bidding has finished find out

- how many people bought back their particular object
- how many people bought more than one thing
- whether anyone bought nothing
- who spent the most
- who spent the least

6 Finally encourage learners to discuss why they decided to pay what
   they did for different things, or why they decided not to buy.

Writing follow-on

a Choose an object that you own but rather dislike and write an advert
   emphasizing its positive qualities, suitable for placing in a local shop
   window. For example, an advert for a rather old children's bike might
   look as follows:

For Sale

Children's bicycle for sale. A good first bike for a boy between 4 & 6 years. Attractive yellow paintwork. Strong tyres and good brakes. Simple design and easy to store. Can deliver.

Contact C.A. Bevan on 01234 56789

---

b When everybody has finished, place the adverts around the room and give learners time to browse and to note down any articles they are particularly interested in.

c Finally, ask learners to form groups of about four or five and to compare what they are interested in buying.

5.3 Role and language

State and attitude

Language focus   Casual conversation

Level   Lower-intermediate upwards

Materials   Role cards

Procedure

FOR ADULTS AND TEENAGERS

1 Write on the board (giving or eliciting) a list of contrasting types, or human conditions.
Some examples might include:

old person   . . . .   young person
lazy person   . . . .   energetic person
thin person   . . . .   fat person

Allocate pairs roles using role cards. For ready-to-use examples, see Box 16.

2 Now write a topic of frequent and casual conversation on the board, something like the weather, the price of clothes / food, the state of our schools, traffic problems.

3 Take two contrasting roles not being used by the learners and then model them both to get the activity off the ground.

4 Pairs now hold a conversation on the agreed topic with each person

in their role. A conversation in an upper-intermediate group between an old and young person on *traffic problems*, for example, might run as follows:

Old:	Look at all these cars!
Young:	And most of them've only got one person in them!
Old:	In my day, we used to cycle everywhere – or walk.
Young:	I suppose people need to travel further these days.
Old:	If you ask me, half of them are too lazy to go anywhere without the car.
Young:	Oh, I don't know about that.

Box 16 Role and language

lazy person . . . . energetic person

happy person . . . . sad person

thin person . . . . fat person

slow person . . . . quick person

pessimistic person . . . . optimistic person

excitable person . . . . calm person

quiet person . . . . chatty person

superficial person . . . . deep-thinking person

lively person . . . . dull person

rich person . . . . poor person

successful person . . . . unsuccessful person

educated person . . . . uneducated person

old person . . . . young person

teacher . . . . student

parent . . . . child

older sibling . . . . younger sibling

uncle/aunt . . . . niece/nephew

shopkeeper . . . . customer

motorist . . . . pedestrian

driver . . . . passenger

grandparent . . . . grandchild

pet-lover . . . . pet-hater

sporty person . . . . non-sporty person

city person . . . . country person

5.4 Desirable qualities

Talking about the best and worst in human nature

Language focus Adjectives to describe types of people

Level Lower-intermediate upwards

Materials Board and paper

Preparation Revise adjectives

Procedure

FOR ADULTS AND TEENAGERS

1 Read out the set of adjectives for the level you are working with (there are ready-to-use sets in Box 17) and ask learners to raise their hands to indicate whether they consider it a positive quality. Check that everyone understands the meaning of all of them, and clarify any possible ambiguities (e.g. thoughtful – someone who likes thinking, or someone who is considerate?).

2 Write the adjectives appropriate to your learners' level on the board.

3 Ask learners to choose the four words from their set that they would most like to apply to them, and to rank them in order of importance from 1 to 4, 1 being the most important. A lower-intermediate result might look like this:

```
1 – happy
2 – kind
3 – generous
4 – intelligent
```

4 Now ask them to write down and put a cross next to any words they would not wish to apply to them. Again, a lower-intermediate result might look like this:

```
greedy   x
boring   x
careless   x
shy   x
nasty   x
```

5 Now ask the class to choose from the same set the four features they

89

would most wish for in a friend. Again, ask everyone to rank these, this time using letters *a–d* in order of importance, *a* being the most important, and to write down and draw a circle next to the qualities they would not like their friend to have. For example:

a – funny	boring o
b – thoughtful	formal o
c – honest	nasty o
d – kind	forgetful o
	greedy o

6 Ask learners to work with a partner and to compare their opinions, giving reasons.

Box 17 Desirable qualities

Lower-intermediate adjectives

friendly, cheerful, greedy, calm, kind, loving, funny, gentle, thoughtful, boring, formal, nasty, brave, generous, wise, helpful, forgetful, careless, honest, shy, strong

Upper-intermediate adjectives

sociable, approachable, relaxed, ambitious, deep, blunt, respectful, determined, selfish, distant, uptight, nervous, self-conscious, uninspiring, quarrelsome, amusing, straightforward, responsible, rough, proud, charming

Advanced adjectives

cultured, witty, sneaky, driven, antagonistic, sly, pedantic, shallow, charitable, highly strung, nonconformist, aggressive, compassionate, altruistic, sharp, ambitious, approachable, controlled, upstanding, self-confident, narrow, passionate

---

5.5 What's important in a teacher?

Describing important qualities in teachers

Language focus   Adjectives to describe teachers
Level   Intermediate upwards
Materials   Board

Procedure

FOR ADULTS AND TEENAGERS

1 Write the word *teachers* on the board and ask learners to volunteer any words that occur to them in connection with *teachers*. Don't write them down at this stage.
2 Now divide the board into two, and write two headings – *good* on one side, and *bad* on the other. Elicit any words or phrases that learners associate with good or bad teachers, and this time write down a few on each side.
3 Now give learners the list of positive adjectives in Box 18 that could be used to describe a well-liked teacher of theirs. Ask them to work individually and to circle at least five qualities that they could apply to a past teacher they really enjoyed learning with. They may add any adjectives they feel are missing.
4 In pairs, give them time to tell each other which qualities they circled and to tell each other about their well-liked teacher.
5 Finally, ask learners to choose the one quality they consider essential for a good teacher, and finish off with a round starting *I think a good teacher has to be . . . .*

Writing follow-on

a Give learners a negative adjective sheet (see Box 18) and ask them to recall a teacher they really didn't like.
b Learners should choose at least five adjectives and incorporate them into a piece of writing describing the teacher and why they didn't like him/her.

Box 18   What's important in a teacher?

Positive adjectives

Easier

hardworking, motivating, fun, kind, clever, interesting, unusual, caring, fair, friendly

More difficult

industrious, inspiring, dedicated, humorous, committed, democratic, dynamic, inventive, knowledgeable, approachable

Negative adjectives

Easier

dull, boring, lazy, unfair, unkind, unhelpful, nasty, cruel, mean, bullying

More difficult

dictatorial, tyrannical, vindictive, spiteful, humiliating, uncharitable, incompetent, bigoted, sadistic, uncooperative

---

Acknowledgement

We first encountered the idea of working with memories of teachers at a workshop with Christine Frank.

5.6 Qualities for life

Deciding what qualities help you get the best out of life

....

Language focus   Words and phrases used for describing qualities that enhance enjoyment of life

Level   Intermediate upwards

Materials   Board

....

Procedure

FOR ADULTS AND TEENAGERS

1 Ask the class to think of things about themselves and others that enhance their enjoyment of life. They may be personality traits (e.g. a good sense of humour), abilities (e.g. the ability to sing), or attributes (e.g. intelligence).

2 After a few minutes, brainstorm these, writing up as many as the class can think of and you have space for on the board.
3 Ask learners to choose one quality only (from the board, or that they subsequently think of), that they consider would enhance their own enjoyment of life. They should tell nobody at this stage.
4 The teacher chooses a quality and pretends to hold it in her hands. She chooses a learner and gives them the quality as a present, saying, e.g.

Teacher: Vali – I'd like to give you the ability to sing if you don't already have it.

The learner replies, saying, e.g.

Vali: Thank you – and I'd like to give you the ability to control your emotions in difficult situations.

The teacher thanks the learner, takes the new gift in his or her hands and then looks for someone to pass the new gift on to, so the next exchange goes:

Teacher: Margit – I'd like to give you the ability to control your emotions in difficult situations.
Margit: Thank you – I'd like to give you a good sense of humour.

with learner and teacher holding and passing on the gifts.
5 When learners understand that you give your first gift away to get a new one which you then give away, and so on, ask everybody to stand up and walk around exchanging 'gifts'. When everybody has spoken to most other people, ask learners to return to their seats.
6 To round off on a positive note, ask learners which of all the gifts they were given they would most like to keep. If you think your class can take rejection, you may also ask if there are any they would like to throw away.

Acknowledgement

This is based on an idea by Kathy Keohane, first published in *Modern English Teacher* Volume 4, October 1995.

Writing follow-on

a Tell your learners the first part of the Fairy Tale 'Sleeping Beauty' (notes for this can be found at the end of this activity) where the fairies are summoned to bestow gifts on the Royal Princess. Include the potentially fatal gift of the uninvited fairy.
b Ask learners to write a modern-day version of this part of the story,

thinking of what qualities a child (boy or girl, depending on their choice) would find most useful in life and why. Ask them to indicate one quality which they would not wish on a child – i.e. that would diminish the quality of life.

Notes for 'The Sleeping Beauty' (first part)

long ago a King and Queen longed for a child

baby daughter born after waiting many years

held a big party – invited seven fairies

fairies gave gifts – beauty / good nature / grace / art of dancing / beautiful voice / ability to play any musical instrument

suddenly an old, cross fairy came in – furious because she had not been invited

put a curse on the baby so that she would die on her sixteenth birthday

seventh fairy had not had her turn, and could not stop the curse but could soften it.

A Modern Day Sleeping Beauty

A friend of mine asked me if I would like to be her new son's Godmother. I was delighted, particularly because I was going to be able to choose six qualities to help him with life in the twenty-first century. After some thought, these were the qualities I chose:

the ability to form good relationships – good friends and happy families make life easy and rewarding

a sense of humour – helps in all sorts of situations

an openness to learning – because things will be changing ever faster in the 21st century

the ability to make money – because money makes life comfortable

the ability to relax – in a fast world it's important to be able to slow down

confidence – you need this to achieve what you are capable of

There are many undesirable qualities, but I think I would choose 'greed' as the one I would least like him to have in the 21st century. I think a lot of people are greedy and it makes them very dissatisfied in life.

5.7 Treasured possessions

The emotional value of material things

This activity is closely related to 5.6, but centres on objects rather than personal qualities or attributes. It also has features in common with activities 5.1 and 5.2.

Language focus   Detailed description of objects

Level   Intermediate upwards

Materials   Paper

Preparation   It may be useful to ask learners to think of and describe a possession before this lesson.

Procedure

FOR ADULTS AND TEENAGERS

1 Ask learners to think of a treasured possession which they would be happy to show and talk about to others. When they have thought, ask them to write a short but detailed description of it, e.g.

> It's a small, squat blue and white milk-jug. The pattern is made up of very small blurred dots of blue and the rim is dark blue.

Help learners with their language as they are writing. Allow dictionaries.

2 Now tell learners that they are going to give their object to somebody else to look at. Start as with Activity 5.6, with the teacher 'giving' their object to someone and 'receiving' the learner's object in return. The description should be incorporated into the giving of the object, but does not have to be exactly the same as the written description, e.g.

3 The teacher then passes on the learner's gift to someone else, taking care to describe it as it was described to her, and the learner passes on the teacher's gift, and so on. When everybody has talked to most other people, ask learners to return to their seats with the last gift they received.

4 To conclude the activity, ask learners to describe their original object to the class and, if they wish, to say why it is important to them. After each learner has spoken, the person who now has that gift should walk to the original owner to return it. It is then their turn to describe their object. For example:

Teacher: I described a small, squat blue and white jug which has a pattern made up of blurred dots. It's actually very ordinary and cheap, but I treasure it because it was one of the last things my father gave me before he died. It used to have a teapot to match, but unfortunately that broke.

Zara: I've got your jug! Here it is!

Teacher: Thanks.

Zara: I described a tiny model aeroplane that is so small . . .

Writing follow-on

a Ask learners to divide a piece of paper into two. Learners should choose from their own belongings and, on the left of the paper, list, in order, ten of their possessions from the most to the least expensive.

b In the right-hand column, learners should write something about how important the object is to them. An abridged list can be seen below.

OBJECT	IMPORTANCE
computer	very important – can't work without it
CD player	can't do without it – I need to listen to my music
pencil	not important in itself – but pencils are important to have, in order to write
home-made calendar	I want to keep it for ever – my little brother made it for me.

c Ask them to bring their lists to class. Display them so that others can see what's been written.
d When everybody has had a look, ask them to sit in small groups and to think about what the lists say about their personal values.

5.8 Deserving causes

Persuasion

Language focus   Persuading through writing

Level   Upper-intermediate upwards

Materials   Box 19 handout

Preparation   Useful to have background knowledge of charity types

Procedure

FOR ADULTS AND TEENAGERS

1 Give learners a list of 'causes'. Use your own or choose from Box 19 at the end of the activity. Ask them to look through and decide how likely they as individuals would be to contribute to them financially.
2 Pair learners and ask them to compare their results. Give them plenty of time to explain their reasons.
3 Explain to the class that all these causes successfully raise funds in Britain, and that they do this in different ways, for example, collecting from door to door, advertising in the press, sending out individual letters asking for money, and advertising on billboards.
4 Ask pairs to consider one of the causes that they feel would be difficult to raise money for. Ask them to work together to produce a piece of writing to help raise funds for that cause. Formats to choose from which are regularly used for this purpose could include:
   • an individual letter
   • a poster
   • a promotional leaflet
   • a newspaper advert

Give just
£2 a month
and help people
work themselves
out of poverty.

£2 a month can give a poor family the seeds and tools they
need. With hard work it is an investment that will grow, helping
people to help themselves long into the future.

People in the third world don't want to live on hand-outs.
With your help they won't have to.

5 Learners can be encouraged to illustrate their writing, or to use
imaginative formatting.

Box 19 Deserving causes

DESERVING CAUSES?

Would you give money. . .

a   so that your school (or your children's school) could buy more books and computers?

b   so that seriously ill children with a specific disease could have better medical care?

c   to help another nation cope with a national disaster (e.g. an earthquake, flood or famine)?

d   to help dogs and cats who have been mistreated and abandoned?

e   to help train guide dogs in order that blind people can be more independent?

f   to help an individual you know (not a member of your family) afford essential medical care?

g   so that a rescue organization could afford to buy more rescue equipment?

h   so that old people are better cared for in your society?

i   to help educate an indvidual child from a nation poorer than yours?

j   so that an important art treasure would remain in a national museum and not go to a foreign buyer?

k   to help people who have a problem with alcohol to stop drinking?

l   in order to preserve an endangered species of animal?

m   to provide better care for people who are terminally ill and need a dignified place to end their lives?

n   in order to preserve an endangered species of plant?

o   to support a particular political party in your country's elections?

6 Self-knowledge and knowledge of others

6.1 My past, my self

Knowledge of past self

Language focus   Question practice; reported speech

Level   Intermediate upwards

Materials   Strips of paper to pin to each learner

Preparation   Cutting strips of paper

Procedure

FOR ADULTS AND TEENAGERS

1 Ask learners to think back to when they were a particular age, say 15/16, when important events occur (e.g. exam results). With teenagers, ask them to think back just a couple of years. Ask learners to think of a person older than them who knew them well at that time. They might choose a parent, another relative, or a teacher. Give them a few moments to think about what that person thought of them at that age.
2 Tell the learners that this person is at a party where everybody is talking about young people. Learners attach to themselves a piece of paper with 'their' adult's name on it and the role that person had in relation to them. For example:

Valerie Masters
Kathy's maths
teacher

3 They then circulate. Learners greet each other using the adults' names, then ask after the 'children'. Model appropriate questions and lines of inquiry if necessary. For example:

> How's Kathy?
> Is she working hard for her exam?
> Does she need to pass maths to get into college?
> Is she easy to teach?
> Is she weak in all subjects, or is it just maths?

Take part yourself as an adult who knew you at 15.
4 After the activity has run its course, learners return to their seats and do a round beginning *I think . . . thought I was . . . when I was 15, but/and I . . .* Begin yourself. For example:

I think Miss Valerie Masters thought I was lazy when I was 15, but I know I wasn't. I was just not very good at maths!

Follow-on for upper-intermediate upwards

Learners form small groups (say three or four per group) and discuss in more detail the people they chose to be and their relationship with them in the past. For example:

I chose to be Valerie Masters, my maths teacher. She thought I was lazy. This made it difficult for me to like her at all. In fact, I made sure there was a big distance between us and . . .

Follow-on 2 for upper-intermediate upwards

For homework, learners might like to write a short piece on how they felt during the time in their life they have discussed in class. For example:

> I felt very trapped at school when I was around 15 years old. I had to study a lot of subjects I had no interest in. I wasn't at all clear about what I wanted to do with my life and I felt quite unhappy at school, particularly in lessons which I found difficult. Really I just wanted to be with my friends, enjoying myself.

Follow-on 3 for upper-intermediate upwards

A 'compare and contrast' piece of writing could follow on from this, with learners writing about two people who had very different views of them at a fixed point in the past. It could be two adults, or it might be the views of adults vs. friends. For example:

> I'm sure my art teacher and my maths teacher had very different opinions of me. I found maths so hard. Art lessons, on the other hand, were one of my favourites. I used to ask for homework! So to my art teachers I seemed very industrious, whereas my maths teacher thought I was just lazy and fairly useless.

6.2 Changes

Discussing significant life experiences

Language focus   Question practice

Level   Lower-intermediate upwards

Procedure

FOR ADULTS AND TEENAGERS

1 Write a sentence on the board about a positive change that has taken place in your life, for example, *In 1973 my daughter was born.*
2 Taking a 'hot seat' in the middle of the group, ask the class to ask you some questions about your statement. Questions for the statement above might run as follows:

> – Where was she born?
> – Did she look like you or your wife?
> – Who does she look like now?
> – Was she your first child?
> – Before she was born, did you want the baby to be a boy or a girl?
> – What did you call her?
> – Who chose the name – you or your wife?
> – Was she an easy baby to look after?

3 Give the learners a few minutes to think of their own important changes: ones they are willing to share with the class. They should tell their partner what their change is and work in pairs to prepare themselves for the main activity. Each learner asks their partner as many questions as they can about the other's change.
4 Then, taking the hot seat, they introduce their event to the class and

answer questions. Nobody should be in the hot seat for more than two minutes.

Writing follow-on

a   Write this phrase on the board:

I can remember the first time I . . .

and ask learners to volunteer ways of finishing the sentence using episodes from their own lives. Write down all the ideas, including some of your own if you wish. Your board may include some of the following:

went on holiday / went to school / rode a bike / played the piano / met my best friend / smoked a cigarette / went on an aeroplane / had a music lesson

b   When the board is full enough, ask learners to choose one of the endings and to write the full sentence at the top of a clean sheet of paper. For example:

I can remember the first time I met my best friend.

c   They then pass this to the person on their right, who writes a question about the sentence, and then passes the paper on to someone else, who writes another question, and so on. The finished paper will be full of questions. Some examples for *met my best friend* can be found below.

> Did you like him/her when you very first saw him/her?
> What did you think when you first met him/her?
> Where were you when you met?
> How old were you when you met?
> What was your best friend wearing?

d   These completed papers, full of questions, are returned to the person who wrote the original sentence. They should then write a short passage incorporating the answers to the questions, using their initial sentence (in the case of the example, *The first time I met my best friend*). These pieces of writing can then be displayed in class for everyone to read.

For children

This activity is likely to be more successful if you brainstorm important events with young learners. The birth of a sibling, perhaps, or a special holiday are possible ideas.

6.3 Life maps

Judging the listener's interest

Language focus   The past
Level   Intermediate upwards
Materials   Highway Code symbols

Procedure

This activity spans two lessons

FOR ADULTS AND TEENAGERS

Lesson one

1   Give learners the set of symbols on road maps and signs (cross-roads, hospital, roundabout, scenic road, danger, etc.) from Box 20. Go through the symbols making sure that everyone understands them and encourage learners to add any they feel should be included.
2   Now ask them to think about their lives since birth and to consider how any of these symbols might apply to their own lives. Having done this, they can then be encouraged to devise symbols to account for parts of their life not covered by conventional symbols.
3   For homework, each learner draws a road map of their life, beginning at birth and plotting the journey until now. They may choose to insert some text as in the example.

Lesson two

4   With the maps remaining secret, learners work in pairs. The aim is for them to tell each other their life stories. They should include only what they feel their partner will find interesting. Give them a time limit of two minutes.
5   At the end of the activity, learners show each other their life maps and discuss what they included, what they left out and why. At this stage, you may like to give learners a few minutes to ask each other any questions they may have.
6   Round off by continuing maps into the future.

Example of Life Map

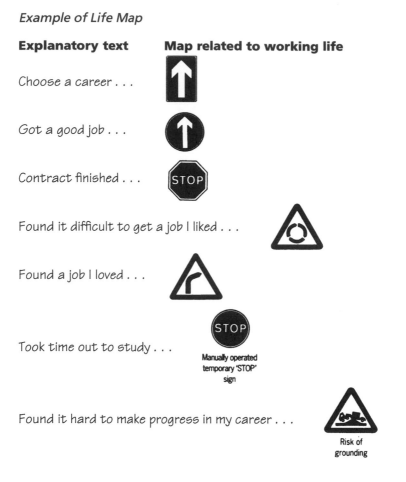

Explanatory text   **Map related to working life**

Choose a career . . .

Got a good job . . .

Contract finished . . .

Found it difficult to get a job I liked . . .

Found a job I loved . . .

Took time out to study . . .

Manually operated
temporary 'STOP'
sign

Found it hard to make progress in my career . . .

Risk of
grounding

Variation 1

Proceed as above, but at stage 4, work with roles, e.g. 'boss and employee', 'stranger and stranger', and a context, e.g. 'at an interview', 'on a train'. These could be brainstormed in advance and learners could choose for themselves.

Variation 2

The activity can also be carried out by learners representing their lives, or aspects of their lives, in other ways, for example a line graph with a negotiated scale (good/bad, difficult/easy), a pie chart, or a picture.

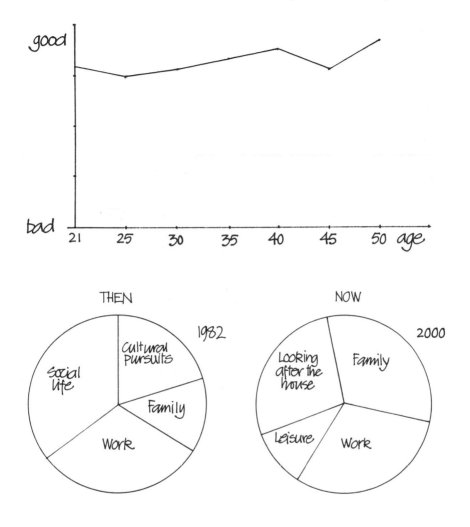

Box 20 Life maps

Signs and symbols

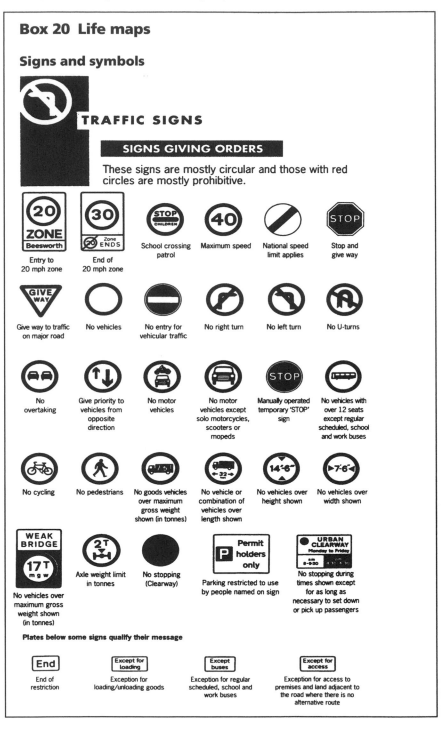

TRAFFIC SIGNS

SIGNS GIVING ORDERS

These signs are mostly circular and those with red circles are mostly prohibitive.

Entry to 20 mph zone

End of 20 mph zone

School crossing patrol

Maximum speed

National speed limit applies

Stop and give way

Give way to traffic on major road

No vehicles

No entry for vehicular traffic

No right turn

No left turn

No U-turns

No overtaking

Give priority to vehicles from opposite direction

No motor vehicles

No motor vehicles except solo motorcycles, scooters or mopeds

Manually operated temporary 'STOP' sign

No vehicles with over 12 seats except regular scheduled, school and work buses

No cycling

No pedestrians

No goods vehicles over maximum gross weight shown (in tonnes)

No vehicle or combination of vehicles over length shown

No vehicles over height shown

No vehicles over width shown

No vehicles over maximum gross weight shown (in tonnes)

Axle weight limit in tonnes

No stopping (Clearway)

Parking restricted to use by people named on sign

No stopping during times shown except for as long as necessary to set down or pick up passengers

Plates below some signs qualify their message

End of restriction

Exception for loading/unloading goods

Exception for regular scheduled, school and work buses

Exception for access to premises and land adjacent to the road where there is no alternative route

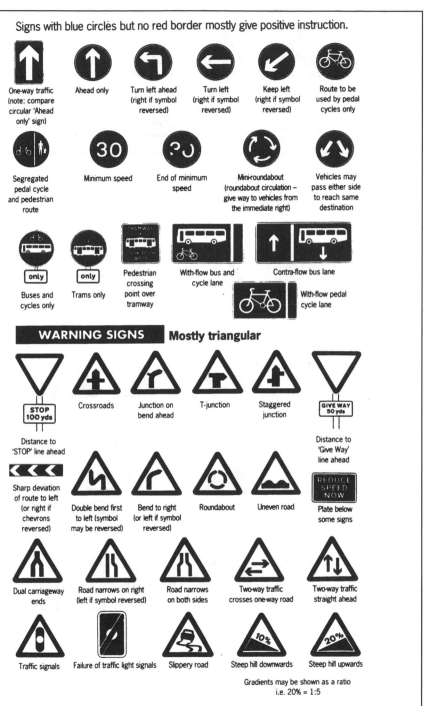

Signs with blue circles but no red border mostly give positive instruction.

One-way traffic (note: compare circular 'Ahead only' sign)

Ahead only

Turn left ahead (right if symbol reversed)

Turn left (right if symbol reversed)

Keep left (right if symbol reversed)

Route to be used by pedal cycles only

Segregated pedal cycle and pedestrian route

Minimum speed

End of minimum speed

Mini-roundabout (roundabout circulation – give way to vehicles from the immediate right)

Vehicles may pass either side to reach same destination

Buses and cycles only

Trams only

Pedestrian crossing point over tramway

With-flow bus and cycle lane

Contra-flow bus lane

With-flow pedal cycle lane

WARNING SIGNS   **Mostly triangular**

Distance to 'STOP' line ahead

Crossroads

Junction on bend ahead

T-junction

Staggered junction

Distance to 'Give Way' line ahead

Sharp deviation of route to left (or right if chevrons reversed)

Double bend first to left (symbol may be reversed)

Bend to right (or left if symbol reversed)

Roundabout

Uneven road

Plate below some signs

Dual carriageway ends

Road narrows on right (left if symbol reversed)

Road narrows on both sides

Two-way traffic crosses one-way road

Two-way traffic straight ahead

Traffic signals

Failure of traffic light signals

Slippery road

Steep hill downwards

Steep hill upwards

Gradients may be shown as a ratio i.e. 20% = 1:5

109

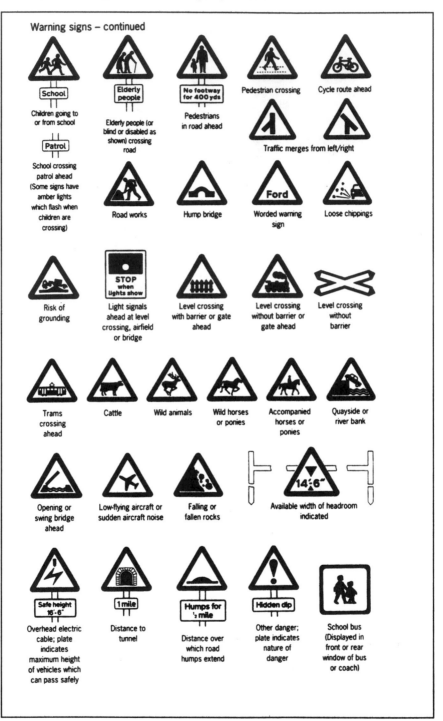

Warning signs – continued

Children going to or from school

School crossing patrol ahead (Some signs have amber lights which flash when children are crossing)

Elderly people (or blind or disabled as shown) crossing road

Pedestrians in road ahead

Pedestrian crossing

Cycle route ahead

Traffic merges from left/right

Road works

Hump bridge

Worded warning sign

Loose chippings

Risk of grounding

Light signals ahead at level crossing, airfield or bridge

Level crossing with barrier or gate ahead

Level crossing without barrier or gate ahead

Level crossing without barrier

Trams crossing ahead

Cattle

Wild animals

Wild horses or ponies

Accompanied horses or ponies

Quayside or river bank

Opening or swing bridge ahead

Low-flying aircraft or sudden aircraft noise

Falling or fallen rocks

Available width of headroom indicated

Overhead electric cable; plate indicates maximum height of vehicles which can pass safely

Distance to tunnel

Distance over which road humps extend

Other danger; plate indicates nature of danger

School bus (Displayed in front or rear window of bus or coach)

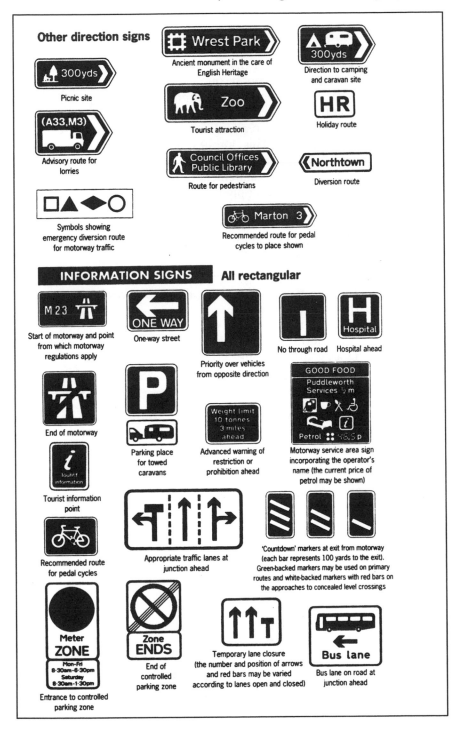

Other direction signs

Wrest Park
Ancient monument in the care of
English Heritage

300yds
Direction to camping
and caravan site

300yds
Picnic site

Zoo
Tourist attraction

HR
Holiday route

(A33,M3)
Advisory route for
lorries

Council Offices
Public Library
Route for pedestrians

Northtown
Diversion route

Symbols showing
emergency diversion route
for motorway traffic

Marton 3
Recommended route for pedal
cycles to place shown

INFORMATION SIGNS   **All rectangular**

M 23
Start of motorway and point
from which motorway
regulations apply

ONE WAY
One-way street

Priority over vehicles
from opposite direction

No through road

H
Hospital
Hospital ahead

End of motorway

P
Parking place
for towed
caravans

Weight limit
10 tonnes
3 miles
ahead
Advanced warning of
restriction or
prohibition ahead

GOOD FOOD
Puddleworth
Services ½ m
Petrol ∷ 45.5 p
Motorway service area sign
incorporating the operator's
name (the current price of
petrol may be shown)

i
tourist
information
Tourist information
point

Appropriate traffic lanes at
junction ahead

'Countdown' markers at exit from motorway
(each bar represents 100 yards to the exit).
Green-backed markers may be used on primary
routes and white-backed markers with red bars on
the approaches to concealed level crossings

Recommended route
for pedal cycles

Meter
ZONE
Mon–Fri
8·30am–6·30pm
Saturday
8·30am–1·30pm
Entrance to controlled
parking zone

Zone
ENDS
End of
controlled
parking zone

Temporary lane closure
(the number and position of arrows
and red bars may be varied
according to lanes open and closed)

Bus lane
Bus lane on road at
junction ahead

Follow-on

a Ask learners to think of something really positive about themselves (e.g. helpful son, diligent worker, kind father, good at sport, keen cook, etc.). The achievement must not be one already known or mentioned.

b Give learners a slip of paper each upon which they write their thought. Collect these papers in.

c Using the room as a gauge, read out one of the statements. One end of the room represents 'This applies to me' and the other end represents 'This is not me at all.'

d The teacher reads out the statements to learners who listen and consider whether this could apply to them. When they have decided, they go and stand wherever they feel is the most appropriate place.

e When this stage is finished, ask learners to form groups of three or four in which they can talk about their own positive statements with each other. For example:

Judit:	I'm a keen cook. I'm also quite a good cook – and am quite proud of this!
Zsuzsa:	What sort of things do you make?
Judit:	A lot of traditional Hungarian dishes.
Zoltan:	Does your family like your food?
Judit:	Oh yes! They have to!

f Finally, do a quick round where everybody in turn gets a chance to say their original statement to the whole class.

FOR CHILDREN

Language focus   Practice in talking about the past and the present

Procedure

1 Give children a set of signs. Ask them to choose one or two to say something about their own lives. For example:

I've got a bicycle.

My sister went to hospital yesterday.

There are two children in my family.

2 Go round helping. When everyone has got the idea, ask them to write one or two more pieces of information for each sign. For example:

I've got a bicycle. It's yellow. I can ride it very well.

My sister went to hospital yesterday. She had her eyes tested. She brought me a word-search book.

There are two children in my family. My sister is 5. I am 8.

6.4 Personal coat of arms

Representing yourself in a badge

Language focus   Noun phrases

Level   Lower-intermediate upwards

Materials   Sheets of paper

Preparation   Explain the origins of coats of arms and pre-teach the expression 'coat of arms'

Procedure

FOR ADULTS AND TEENAGERS

1 Ask learners to design their own, largely pictorial, coat of arms according to the instructions below. Help them understand what such a coat of arms might look like by showing them an example, preferably about yourself. Set a time limit and ask learners not to put their own names on their work.

Instructions for coat of arms contents:

- something from my past which is important to me
- something which is important to me now
- something that symbolizes me
- my ambition

This example of a coat of arms using those instructions has flags to show where its creator's ancestors came from, a picture of children playing to show what's important to that person now, a terrier dog to show that this person is determined and won't give up until they've

113

got what they want, and a picture of an open book being written to show that their ambition is to write a good book.

2 When the time limit is up, display the coats of arms around the room. Ask learners to see if they can guess whose is which as they walk around and look at each other's work.
3 Finally, ask learners to go and stand by their own piece of work.

Follow-on

In groups of two or three, ask learners to design a coat of arms for the institution or school you are in. Display and invite comment.

Variation

For learners who are reluctant to divulge this sort of information about themselves, provide alternative instructions, e.g.

my favourite food, my favourite music, my favourite animal, a country I want to visit, my zodiac sign, favourite type of transport, etc.

Variation for upper-intermediate to advanced learners

Use the following instructions, pre-teaching *motto* and *epitaph*:

biggest success, biggest failure, hope for this year, favourite animal or personal symbol, hope for ten years hence, motto, epitaph

Below is an example of Griff's coat of arms based on the above instructions.

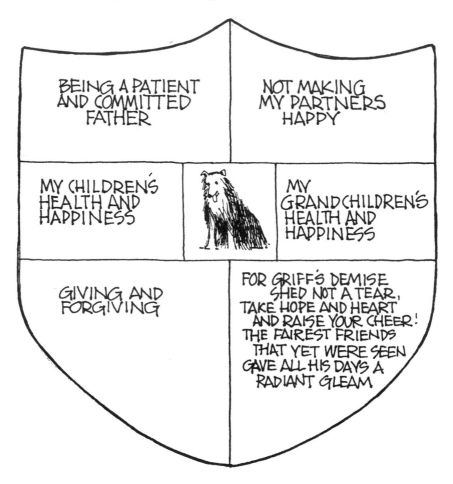

Follow-on

Create seven points in the classroom which correspond to the seven boxes in the coat of arms (that is, turn the classroom into the seven areas, one for success, one for failure, one for hope for this year, etc.) Ask them to go to their favourite area, and then tell someone else in the same place what they have written in that box and why. Finally, ask them to go to their least favourite area and do the same.

6.5 True short stories

Talking about true-life incidents

Language focus   Narrating true stories
Level   Lower-intermediate upwards

Procedure

FOR ADULTS AND TEENAGERS

1 Arrange the seating so that you create a number of train compartments, with learners facing each other in pairs.
2 Tell learners that they are on a long and boring train journey, and have agreed to relate one important incident in their lives to the other passengers in five minutes. Give them time to think before they start, and emphasize that neither questions nor discussion are allowed.

Follow-on

When learners have finished relating their stories, form new groups of four, consisting of two lots of original pairs. Learners then have to tell the new group the story they were told by the partner who is still with them in the new group, whilst the person whose story it is listens on and makes a mental note of how accurate the retelling is. When all the retellings are finished, the 'owners' of the stories tell the 'retellers' how accurate they feel the new rendition was.

Acknowledgement

We encountered the way of working with retelling stories in the follow-on from Julian Edge.

6.6 Colours

Accurate description of colours

This activity spans two lessons

Language focus   Vocabulary describing shades of colour

Level   Lower-intermediate upwards

Materials   Sheets of paper

Preparation   Lesson two is only truly successful if the lesson one homework task is completed

---

Procedure

FOR ADULTS AND TEENAGERS

Lesson one

1 At the end of class create a line-up in which one end of the class represents red, the other violet, and the space in between is the remaining colours of the spectrum (orange, yellow, green, blue and indigo). Learners place themselves on their favourite part of the colour spectrum.

2 Ask each learner to choose a colour and to note down everything they see which is that colour for the rest of the day. They should note a) the object and b) the shade of the colour. Ask them to bring a coloured pencil of 'their' colour to the next class.

Lesson two

3 In the next class, give learners a clean sheet of A4 paper which they should fold in two. On one side of the paper, ask them to write down, using their coloured pencil, everything they noted down. On the other side, using their coloured pencil, they should write as many words as they can which they associate with their chosen colour. Below is an example from a sheet for 'green'.

Objects seen:	Words I associate with the colour green:
deep green grass	fresh
pale green leaves	natural
jade green beads	calming
olive green T-shirt	soothing
sparkling green emerald	healthy
dull green canvas	fertile
	healing

4 When everyone has finished, display the sheets around the room for everyone to walk around and look at. Ask them to write down any words or phrases they particularly like the sound of from some of the colour sheets they see.
5 Finish off with a round where learners say a word or phrase they particularly liked that they saw on someone else's colour sheet.

Follow-on

These sheets, and the notes made in stage 4, can be used to provide ideas for learners to write some short colour poems.

FOR CHILDREN

Lesson one

1 At the end of class, create a colour line-up, as for adults and teenagers, and ask learners to place themselves on the part of the line which represents their favourite colour.
2 Ask them to go home and find three smallish things, or pictures of things they like which are predominantly in their favourite colour.

Lesson two

3 Group learners according to their favourite colour. They should show each other the objects and pictures they have brought and then place them all together on a desk.
4 With dictionaries and the teacher's help, they should label the objects by writing a) the name of the object and b) its particular colour. Limit the number of shades you include. An example of part of a table for 'yellow' might look like this:

5 Give learners a chance to go round the room looking at the different colour tables. When everybody has had the chance to have a good look, take away the labels.
6 Now the teacher reads out the names of the objects and challenges learners to remember the exact colour of those objects.

6.7 Things I can't do without

Visual representation of things important to individuals

Language focus Question practice; giving a monologue
Level Lower-intermediate upwards
Materials Paper; glue; lots of visuals; a prepared collage
Preparation Compiling the collage

Procedure

FOR ADULTS, TEENAGERS AND CHILDREN

1 Brainstorm 'things I can't do without' on the board. Make sure you include lots of very ordinary things like *pots and pans, coffee*, etc., as well as more exotic needs, such as *holidays abroad*.

2 Check that your students know that a collage is a collection of pictures, or pictures and things, all stuck down together to form a larger picture. Either in class or at home, ask learners to put together a personal collage to show a large number of things they can't do without. You should also make your own collage. If you are working in class, help them with any new vocabulary. If they are compiling their collage at home, ask them to work with dictionaries to make sure they know the names of all they have included.

3 When the collages are complete, show yours to the class and tell them about it. For example:.

This is a picture of a dog. Dogs are very important to me. My dog looks quite a lot like this one and he's a very good friend to me.

Invite learners to ask you questions and to interrupt you at appropriate points to find out anything they want to. For example:

> – Is this your first dog?
> – How many dogs have you owned?
> – Is your dog the same size as that one in the picture?
> – Why are dogs important to you? – I can't stand them!
> – Is your dog well-trained?

4 When you have worked with the class like this for about five minutes or so, ask them to work in groups of three, with one person telling the others about their collage and the others asking questions.

5 When everybody has had a chance to tell others about their collage, display them around the room. Ask each learner to tell the class one

thing that they hadn't known before and that they learnt about someone through the collage.

Writing follow-on

a Learners exchange collages with people they haven't worked with in groups. Give them a few minutes to look at the collage and to think of any questions they would like to ask the creator of this collage about the contents of their work.

b Give learners a set amount of time to write as many questions as they can to the owner of the collage. Help them as they work.

c Learners then give their questionnaire to the person whose collage they have devised the questions for. The owner of the collage chooses five questions he or she is prepared to answer and writes replies.

d These answers can be displayed with the collages for all learners to look at.

Variation

Proceed as for the base activity, but at stage 2, ask learners to put together a collage that represents what they couldn't do without at a point in the past. Then proceed as for the base activity from stages 3 to 5.

Acknowledgement

We encountered the idea of working with collages in this way through a fellow-student, Chitra, at the University of Durham.

6.8 How I used to be

Evaluating past behaviour

Language focus   Adverbs of frequency

Level   Lower-intermediate upwards

Materials   Paper; board

Procedure

FOR ADULTS AND TEENAGERS

1 Ask the class to take a sheet of paper and write the following, copied from the board:

I approve of this	I disapprove of this
always	
. . . .	
often	
. . . .	
sometimes	
. . . .	
rarely	
. . . .	
never	
. . . .	

2 Ask learners to think of themselves in one particular situation at a particular time in their lives. They might choose 'at home', 'at school', 'at work', or 'on holiday' for example. They should then write something to the right of the adverbs of frequency that applies to them in their chosen situation at the time of their life they have specified. They should also indicate with a cross on the line whether they consider the frequency of this behaviour generally good or bad. This is someone's appraisal of themselves at home as a seventeen-year-old:

```
always have an opinion
.X. . . . . . . . . . . . . . . . . . . . . . . . . . . . . . . . . . . . . . . . . . . . . . . . . . . .

            often drink coffee
. . . . . . . . . . . . . . . . . . . . . . X . . . . . . . . . . . . . . . . . . . . . . . . . . . . . .

        sometimes get the tea ready
. . . . . . . . . X . . . . . . . . . . . . . . . . . . . . . . . . . . . . . . . . . . . . . . . . . .

        rarely help around the house
. . . . . . . . . . . . . . . . . . . . . . . . . . . . . . X . . . . . . . . . . . . . . . . . . . . .

        never stay in on a Friday night
. . . . . . . . . . . . . . . . . X . . . . . . . . . . . . . . . . . . . . . . . . . . . . . . . . . .
```

3 Learners then form groups of four in which they show each other their self-assessments and explain why they have marked their crosses where they have.

7 Images and scenes – real and ideal

7.1 The never-ending story

Story-telling

Language focus   Narration

Level   Intermediate upwards

Preparation   Some practice at round-the-class narration

Procedure

FOR ADULTS, TEENAGERS AND CHILDREN

1 Ask the class to think of a theme for a story, e.g. a first trip abroad, a prisoner escapes, the haunted house.
2 Begin the story yourself. In a small class, learners can, in round, add one to three sentences to make a story. The only rules are that learners must stick to the theme.

Follow-on

For homework, ask learners to write the story up, making any changes they want.

Variation 1

Tell the story in role. Begin yourself and try to establish the personality of the teller. In a round, learners add one to three sentences and try to illustrate the character of the teller. You may have to caricature a nervous, boastful or angry teller in your opening.

Variation 2

Instead of using one to three sentences, ask learners to break off at a pertinent point in the text which begs to be continued, for example:

• *but what she didn't know was . . .*

- *until he heard . . .*
- *when all of a sudden . . .*
- *then, out of the darkness . . .*

Variation 3

Provide each learner with a word or picture which they have to weave into their bit of the story.

7.2 The buck stops here

Story-telling

This activity is very similar to 7.1.

Language focus   Narration

Level   Intermediate upwards

Materials   The buck

Procedure

FOR ADULTS, TEENAGERS AND CHILDREN

1 Choose some small object (a dice for example) to represent the buck, and tell the class it gives the holder the right to speak; no-one may say anything unless they are holding it.
2 Start an open-ended story (e.g. *I felt very angry when I read the newspaper*) then pass the buck on: each buck-holder may add not more than two sentences. Learners may pass by passing the buck on, and the buck continues to do the rounds until the story seems to be over or you decide to finish it.

Variation

Gently throw the buck to someone who *must* add to the story, and who then throws it on. Each learner receives the buck only once.

Follow-on

Learners write the story up for homework; they can make any changes they wish, and the only part that must stay constant is the opening line. If they are interestingly different, the stories can then be displayed and read by the class.

7.3 Unusual life experiences

Speaking confidently in public

Language focus   Sequencing events

Level   Intermediate upwards

Procedure

FOR ADULTS AND TEENAGERS

1 Brainstorm 'Unusual episodes in our lives'. These don't have to be too out-of-the-ordinary. Guide learners in terms of themes, e.g. transport, near-misses, relationships, incidents.
2 Tell learners about an unusual episode in your own life. This is a story that happened to one of the authors.

> In the summer of 1992, I was working on a summer school in Durham, where I also lived. I was in the administration office waiting to meet a new colleague. She was a local woman whom we had chosen to employ as a link-up between the summer school and the community. When this person arrived, we were introduced and shook hands. My surname is fairly unusual in England and if it wasn't for that, what followed would probably not have happened. My new colleague asked me if I had been at a particular school in Southampton. I was rather taken aback and said that I had. She then reintroduced herself as a former teacher of mine with whom I had kept in contact after leaving school, but subsequently lost touch. We had both changed a lot physically but still got on really well. I was absolutely delighted and we had a really great three weeks on the course together. And subsequently? Well – we fairly quickly lost touch!

3 When you've told your story, ask the class to think about all the characters in the episode; they should consider why the event might have occurred and what each individual might have been feeling, doing and/or saying at the time of the event and immediately before and after.
4 When this has been completed, ask each learner to think of an unusual episode in their own life. Then put learners into groups of four and ask them to tell each other their stories.
5 The group then agrees on which episode is the most feasible to act out and constructs a mini-drama involving, if possible, all the members of the smaller group. Remember to emphasize that each

character should be aware of a) who they are and b) what they are feeling, doing and saying. After due time for rehearsal, they then enact the scene in front of the entire class.

Writing follow-on

For homework, learners can either:

a write up their own unusual episode;
b write up an unusual episode they saw enacted;
c write up an incident they did not discuss in class.

7.4 Pictures

Describing landscapes

Language focus   Describing landscapes

Level   Intermediate upwards

Materials   Paper and pencil; board

Preparation   Review vocabulary needed for landscape descriptions; supply useful expressions for describing a picture.

Procedure

FOR ADULTS, TEENAGERS AND CHILDREN

1 Draw a large, simple landscape picture on the board to practise useful expressions for describing a picture – *in the background, foreground, top/bottom/left/right, at the side, in the corner, middle . . .* etc.

2 Divide the class into pairs, A and B. Ask As to close their eyes and to think of a scene or landscape that they find particularly restful or beautiful.

3 Now As describe the landscape to Bs, and Bs draw it. (Note that As cannot see what Bs are drawing.)

4 Change roles and do the same again.

5 Now ask each student to give the picture they have drawn a title, and to write three sentences about it.

6 Collect the pictures in. Display them so that they can be seen by everybody and see if learners can recognize their descriptions as drawn and described by their partner.

Writing and reading follow-on

a Ask learners to draw the view from a window they frequently look out of. Set a strict time limit or, alternatively, ask them to do this for homework. They should include as much detail as they can, for example:

131

b When they have all completed this, ask them to look at pictures and
to consider what they do and do not like about the view from their
chosen window. They should then write a description of their view
indicating anything they would like different. Go round helping with
vocabulary. This is a description of the view above.

> From my window I can see a busy road. I would prefer it to be a small,
> quiet road. There is a horrible bungalow opposite me. I would like it to
> disappear and I would like to see an empty garden there. Behind it
> are the rooftops of some old terraced houses. I can see the chimney
> pots. I would like to see the whole of those houses. Behind them I can
> see the beautiful high green hills. There are a few trees on the highest
> hills and I can see the farmhouses in the distance. Beside the ugly
> bungalow, to the left, are some terraced houses which are now used
> as shops. I would like them to be normal houses again. To the right is
> a strange little building that is another shop. I would like a tree to be
> there instead.

c   When everybody has done this, ask learners to pass the descriptions and original picture on to the person on their right. This person then has to read the text and draw the view that the original illustrator would prefer.

7.5 **Writing from pictures**

Collaborative writing task

Language focus   Giving opinions
Level   Upper-intermediate upwards
Materials   Copies of paintings

Procedure

FOR ADULTS AND TEENAGERS

1 Choose a variety of copies of paintings and place them around the room with a piece of A4 paper beside each. There should be about five more pictures than there are learners.
2 Invite learners to walk around and look at the pictures in silence. When they have had a couple of minutes or so to do this, ask them to write any opinions they have about the pictures on the blank paper. They should aim to give opinions on a variety of pictures.
3 When the papers look as though they have a fair number of comments on them, ask learners to sit down. Then randomly distribute the pictures, along with the accompanying comments sheets – one per learner.
4 Now ask learners to write about their painting, incorporating as many of the views expressed on the comments sheets as possible. This may need to extend to a homework task.

Comments on FRANZ MARC (1880–1916)
Little Blue Horse, 1912

> I like it because the horse looks strong.
>
> I like the vivid colours.
>
> The effect of the background is beautiful.
>
> It is like a child's drawing – not clear at all.
>
> This is awful – real horses are much more attractive!
>
> You get a real feeling of the horse being free.
>
> I love it! I want it in my living room!
>
> Blue horses are not for me!

5 In a subsequent lesson, when the writing is ready, display it, with the related pictures, around the room for learners to read. This is an example of a text produced from a painting by Franz Marc:

> This is a picture that inspires different things in different people. Some find the colours and style unsuitable for the subject. They feel that horses are much more attractive in real life! This is probably because the painter uses very particular colours (shades of blue and green) for his horse. Others find the vivid colours and the effect of the background beautiful. Most people, however, like it because it conveys what horses represent to them: strength and freedom.

Variation

If you cannot get copies of paintings, interesting photographs or magazine pictures of any theme (e.g. 'portraits', 'landscapes') work very well.

Acknowledgement

A version of this activity, written by Kathy Keohane, appeared in *Modern English Teacher*, October 1995.

7.6 Months in my life

Associations with times of the year

Language focus   Expressing the past, present and future

Level   Lower-intermediate upwards

Materials   Board; paper

Procedure

FOR ADULTS AND TEENAGERS

Part 1

1 Write the month of your birthday on the board. Ask learners if they associate this month with anything they consider important or that has special meaning for them. It will almost certainly be the month of a student's birthday, wedding anniversary, or some other significant event. Allow anyone for whom this month has special significance to speak. Note down what is said on the board. Make sure you get a good variety of events on the board, and elicit more than just the bare facts, for example:

Vic:	July was always the beginning of the school holidays. I lived far away from everybody and it was hard to get to see people.
Kati:	I first met my husband in July – I didn't find him particularly attractive then!
Gabi:	I'm going to Greece on holiday in July – I'm really looking forward to it.
Juan-Carlos:	We always go to the same place on holiday in July. It was nice when we were young, but now it's getting boring.
Renate:	My first graduation took place in early July – I felt quite proud.
Eija:	My grandfather was born in that month – I really got on well with him.
Maria:	I went to my first pop concert in July – I was 16 years old.
Peter:	I bought a really nice second-hand car last July. I got a really good deal on it.
Imelda:	I just love July because it means the beginning of school holidays.

2 Now ask learners to think of six or seven events that have been significant in their lives and to jot them down, indicating the month in which these events happened. Allow them plenty of time for this, perhaps allocating it for homework, and make it clear that they should include only what they are prepared to share with the class.

Part 2

3 When the information is complete, give each learner a blank sheet of A4 size paper. They should write the name of a month of their own choosing at the top of the paper. Their next task is to do a walkabout activity to find out what other people in the group can remember about the same month. They should note their findings down. Participate yourself.

4 Ask learners to pin up the results or place them on their desks and let people go round and look at what memories people have of particular times of the year.

5 Finally, when everyone is again seated, ask learners to find out more information about one or two more people by asking questions such as:

> Peter – you said you got a really good deal on your car in October. What make was it and how much did you pay?
>
> Renate – you said you graduated in December. What did you study?

7.7 Numbers in my life

Associations with numbers

Language focus   Question, number and fluency practice

Level   Elementary upwards

Materials   Paper and pencil

Preparation   Time to prepare number grid

Procedure

1   In class, or for homework, ask learners to divide a sheet of paper into ten squares. Inside each square, ask them to write a number which is in some way significant to them.

2   When they have finished, on a separate piece of paper, they should write down the significance of the number, taking care to write these in a different order from the original list, and without actually writing the number. This part of the task is likely to include information such as:

house number / car number plate / age / number of rooms in their house / age when they started work/ number of kilometres from home to school, etc.

3   Learners then give their number grid and their explanations of the significance of the number to a partner who uses both sets of information to find out why each number has been included by asking questions, for example:

Does your car number plate have the numbers 145 in it?
Have you got 24 CDs?
Did you meet your best friend when you were 11?

4   When everybody has finished the activity, round off by asking learners to share one piece of information they learned about their partner with the rest of the class.

Variation

A quicker version of this activity involves the teacher calling out a number and asking for anyone to volunteer information about themselves relating to that number, e.g. *Three*:

- My little girl is three.
- I have three sisters.
- I have three siblings.
- I bought three limes at the supermarket today.
- There were three people waiting for the bus with me this morning, etc.

Follow-on

When learners have volunteered information about themselves relating to the number, other learners may ask them questions about this information. For example, if one learner has said *My little girl is three*, others may ask *What's your little girl's name?* etc.

7.8 Feelings

Acting out different moods and feelings

Language focus   Moods and feelings

Level   Intermediate upwards

Materials   Board; strips of paper

Procedure

FOR ADULTS AND TEENAGERS

Part 1

1 Brainstorm 'moods and feelings' on the board. You can contribute words of your own as well, or use ideas from Box 21. When you have done this, ask individuals to look at the words and to match some to situations in their own lives. Give them a few minutes to write down their sentences on strips of paper, then ask for volunteers to share their memories briefly with the rest of the class. Stress that they should only share what they are absolutely comfortable about other

people knowing, because the situations will be used again later. Examples can be seen below.

Sibylle: *I was very relaxed on holiday in September.*
Maha: *I was furious when the music teacher gave me a low mark for something I worked hard on.*
Matti: *I was defiant when my parents said I couldn't go to the fair – I think I'm old enough to go.*
Patxi: *I felt outraged when I saw a mother smacking her small child.*

At the end of this stage, collect in the sentences.

Part 2

2 Divide the class into small groups of three to six members. Give each group one of the sentence strips. Don't give the original speaker their own sentence.

3 Each group then devises a one-minute play which illustrates the situation described; the mini-play may be either silent or with speech, but if spoken, the key word must not be mentioned. The other groups either

   a watch the presentation and after conferring, write their guess on a slip of paper (allow dictionaries) and have the papers collected in to be read out by the teacher or
   b watch and, at the end of the presentation, call out their guesses.

4 Finally, ask if anyone recognized their own situation. If they did, ask them to say briefly how the acted-out version differed from what actually happened.

Box 21 Moods and feelings

Elementary	Intermediate	Advanced
happy	delighted	euphoric
sad	depressed	distressed
afraid	worried	alarmed
angry	furious	displeased
shy	cautious	wary
cross	annoyed	outraged

7.9 **Your image of yourself**

Describing yourself in terms of something else

Language focus   Conditional clauses
Level   Intermediate upwards

Procedure

FOR ADULTS, TEENAGERS AND CHILDREN

1 Write the following questions on the board:

If you were an animal, which animal would you be?
If you were an ice-cream, which flavour would you be?
If you were a colour, which colour would you be?

2 Ask for volunteers to answer these questions orally, and ask learners to say why they have made their answers if they are able. The aim is to choose answers which they feel describe them as they are, rather than as they would like to be. For example:

> – I think I'd probably be a dog, because I'm very loyal.
> – I'd be lemon flavoured because I'm quite sharp.
> – I'd be orange because I'm rather fiery.

3 Elicit more questions from the class and write them up on the board (no more than ten). Ideas for subject areas can include, for example, *a flower / a house / a painting / a building / a song / a country / a town / a plant*. In class, or for homework, ask learners to write down the answers to as many of the questions as they can or would like to, still answering for themselves as they are. They should try to answer a minimum of six.

4 When learners have completed their answers, ask them to form small groups and to compare and discuss their answers.

7.10 A painting of yourself

Describing a picture

Language focus   Prepositions of place; expressions of place

Level   Intermediate upwards

Materials   A5 paper and examples of portraits

Preparation   It may be useful to show the class some portraits of people to give them ideas.

Procedure

FOR ADULTS AND TEENAGERS

Part 1

1 For homework, ask learners to imagine that they have won a competition, the prize for which is to have a famous artist paint their picture. In order to get the picture just right, the artist has requested that the person to be painted do a rough sketch of exactly how they would like to be painted. They should include details such as the background, their position in the picture, what they are wearing, etc. They can write notes on the picture to make sure the artist understands exactly what they want.

Part 2

2 Learners should bring their sketches with them to class. Review prepositions and expressions of place, and then ask half the class to take the role of the commissioned artist, and the other half, the prize-winners. The prize-winners describe their sketch to the artist who has to draw it (still in sketch form) as accurately as possible.
3 Learners then reverse roles.
4 Finally, put up all the pictures around the room and let learners look at them.

8 Closing the course

8.1 Me and the course

Evaluating learning

....

Language focus   Giving opinions
Level   Elementary upwards
Materials   Board

....

Procedure

FOR ADULTS, TEENAGERS AND CHILDREN

1 Brainstorm all the different materials and activities you have used throughout the course. Write up the ideas on the board. They might include some of these:

   coursebook / poems / songs / roleplay / drama / pairwork / worksheets / homework / tapes

2 Tell learners they are going to complete the sentences: *In this class I felt I learned a lot in the lesson when we* . . . and *I felt I didn't learn much in the lesson when we* . . . They can use ideas from the board, or something of their own.

3 Write a heading on the board *The lesson when we* . . . In a circle, if possible, each learner says their complete sentence about what they did/didn't learn well from. Write down what learners say whilst they are speaking, making no distinction between positive and negative comments.

4 Now ask learners to take a piece of paper and to write two separate headings:

   Very helpful   Less helpful

They should aim to use all the ideas on the board and write them under one of the two headings. Results might look something like this:

Very helpful

did the airport roleplay, used the piece of film about the sinking ship, used the video clip about lions, had a whole newspaper to look through, all of us were in the language lab with different cassettes

Less helpful

spent the whole time using dictionaries, used time lines to explain the present perfect, had to invent a make-believe product, did 'the process of how rain is made', watched a complicated video about industry for just a little bit of information

---

5 When they have finished doing this, they should form groups of four and discuss with each other their individual results and consider why they might have found something more or less helpful.

8.2 Unconditional positive regard

Complimenting

....

Language focus   Adjectives and phrases to describe people positively

Level   Intermediate upwards

Materials   Slips of paper; board

Preparation   Cutting up slips of paper with names on

....

Procedure

FOR ADULTS, TEENAGERS AND CHILDREN

1 Ask learners to think of someone they really like a lot, for example a friend or family member, and to think about what it is they like about them. Starting with an example of your own, elicit lots of positive comments about people they are thinking of. Write these on the board. Your board may look something like this:

really good fun / easy to be with / very reliable / kind and generous / very direct / a no-nonsense person / I know where I stand with them / always supportive / very helpful

2 Leave these ideas on the board, and explain that as it is the end of the course, you would like to give learners an opportunity to say some-

thing positive about their fellow course members before the group breaks up.

3 Give each person a slip of paper with the name of another member of the class on it. The recipient has to write a compliment about that person on the slip, using ideas from the board if appropriate or finding something else they want to say. The following are some examples.

Fadhil:	It has always been interesting to listen to this person's intelligent and interesting comments in class.
Abdul Latif:	It's really good having this person in class. He asks all the questions I haven't got the courage to ask!
Ingeborg:	This person has a really good sense of humour – she has made me laugh a lot.
Astrid:	This person is always very helpful.
Georgie:	It's nice to work with this person because she is serious about learning but also good fun.

4 Gather the slips in, jumble them up, and read them out. Learners have to guess a) who it's about and b) who wrote it.

Variation

At point 4, instead of asking learners to guess, simply read out all the compliments.

8.3 Parting gifts

Awareness of personality

Language focus   States of mind and personality traits

Level   Intermediate upwards

Materials   Board

Procedure

FOR ADULTS AND TEENAGERS

1 Brainstorm 'personality traits'. Write them up on the board, e.g. *patient, confident, happy, relaxed, assertive*, etc. There are more ideas in Box 22 at the end of this activity.

2 People choose for themselves what quality they would like as a parting gift.
3 When they have done this, they move around, trying to find other people who chose the same, and share their motives and experiences. For example:

> Imana: I chose 'assertive' because I need it. I think girls need to say what they want and not just do what other people want them to do. But it is hard to be assertive! People don't like it and I have to work hard to have the courage to say what I want.
>
> Kazuo: I chose 'patient'. I think it would be better for me if I could wait for things to happen. I cannot relax when I want something to happen – I want to rush things too often.

Note We have defined the traits as the corresponding adjective (*confident, content*) rather than as the noun (*confidence, contentment*) since adjectives are on the whole simpler and easier for learners to work with.

Variation 1

At stage 2, instead of choosing the gift they would most like, students choose the one they feel they least need. Then continue as above with stage 3.

Variation 2

1 Brainstorm 'personality traits and states of mind' as for the base activity.
2 Give each learner the name of one other person in the class. Ask them to think of a suitable 'parting gift' for this person and to write them a short letter to accompany this gift. Set a time limit. For example:

> Dear Paula
>
> You have a very good sense of humour but you don't let everybody see it. I would like you to be more confident so that you can share your sense of humour with more people.
>
> Best wishes
>
> Marije

146

3 When all the letters are written, ask writers to deliver them person-ally. Give recipients time to read the contents.
4 Finally ask for volunteers to say what they got and whether they were pleased with it. For example:

> Khalid: I got 'content', which is a very nice thing to have, but actually I have it already!
>
> Balthasar: I got 'relaxed'! Maybe I need to learn to be a bit more relaxed because I can never stop doing things!
>
> Rathar: I was given 'open-minded'. I don't like it much. Everybody thinks it's good to be open-minded, but I think you need to have your own ideas about what is right and wrong and to keep to them.

Box 22 Parting gifts

Easier

caring, cheerful, friendly, funny, generous, gentle, happy, hardworking, helpful, honest, kind, lively, loyal, motivated, optimistic, patient, polite, understanding, warm

More difficult

amiable, amusing, assertive, capable, confident, content, courteous, enthusiastic, flexible, good-hearted, industrious, open-minded, outgoing, reasonable, relaxed, reliable, sociable, sympathetic, truthful, witty

---

8.4 Saying thank you

Acknowledging everyone's contributions to the class

....

Language focus Thanking

Level Lower-intermediate upwards

Materials Paper for letter writing

....

Procedure

If you think you want to use this as a 'closing the course' activity, it is a good idea to make a note, throughout the course, of anything you think might be worthy of a thank-you note at the end. Alternatively, write the notes throughout the course but distribute them during the last lesson.

FOR ADULTS, TEENAGERS AND CHILDREN

1 Before class, write a thank-you note to each learner, on a slip of paper, in the form of *Please tell . . . thanks for . . .* You might want to include things like *always being on time / always doing her homework / trying so hard / telling such good jokes in class / being such good fun in lessons / telling us the story about her grandmother*, etc.

2 Distribute the slips, each to a learner not named in the paper, and ask them to deliver the message in the form *I've been asked to thank you for . . .*

3 When all the messages have been delivered, ask each learner to write as many thank-you notes as they can write in five minutes, without naming anyone. They should write fairly short notes on reasonably large pieces of paper as this becomes important in stage 4. Collect these in, redistribute them, and ask each person to read theirs out. Notes may well say things like the examples below:

I'd like to thank you for . . . letting me copy your homework / helping me with my homework / making me laugh / making me feel I'm not the only one who doesn't understand! / having such a great imagination / being my partner in class / picking up my books when I dropped them

---

4 Finally, pin the notes up around the room and let learners walk around and make written guesses on the papers about who wrote them and who they were written to.

8.5 The mood game

Portraying scenes in a particular manner

Language focus   Adjective practice

Level   Lower-intermediate upwards

Materials   Board

Procedure

FOR ADULTS, TEENAGERS AND CHILDREN

1 At the end of the course, when learners are likely to volunteer frank opinions more freely, ask the class to think about some of the ways they have felt during lessons. Ask them to be completely honest with

themselves and to include negative as well as positive feelings. Pool these on the board. You are likely to find words such as *bored, tired, amused, confused, interested, challenged, happy, fed-up, distracted*. Encourage a light-hearted attitude to elicit as many words as possible.

2   One person from each group goes out of the room. Those remaining choose one word or phrase from the board. Encourage them to choose those words that lend themselves most easily to being acted out.

3   The returning person then asks each group member in turn to perform an action 'in the style of the word', e.g. *In the style of the word, shake hands / kiss someone / cross the road / peel a banana / dance the twist*, etc. For example, if the word chosen in stage 2 is *confused*, learners will, in turn, have to perform each of the above commands in a confused manner. Some words are easier than others to enact, and if the person asked can't/won't do it, they say *Pass*. The person asking the question has a complete round to guess the word; then another person goes out.

Variation 1

The class walks round the room while the person who is guessing the word stands in the middle and asks everyone to, e.g. shake hands in the manner of the word.

Variation 2

If your class feels reluctant to volunteer how they feel in your class, you can fill the board with appropriate adjectives first and ask them to choose one or two that represent how they have felt during lessons.

8.6 The course in pictures

Using pictures as an aid to giving opinions

Language focus   Asking questions and giving opinions

Level   Intermediate upwards

Materials   A wide variety of pictures; board

Procedure

FOR ADULTS AND TEENAGERS

1 Have a wide variety of pictures available, all spread out. Learners pick one which represents in some way how they feel about the course they have just been on.
2 Place all the pictures together (on a board or large table) and learners see how the course is visually represented by the group.
3 Learners can speak only one at a time, and can initiate only by asking a question. They can ask about only one picture each. Examples of questions and answers are as follows:

Learner 1:	Who chose the picture of the boat all alone on the water and why?
Learner 2:	I chose it because I felt I was alone on this course, going somewhere but I couldn't see where!
Learner 3:	Who chose the picture of the men leaning over with their heads in barrels?
Learner 4:	I did! I think I'd like to do that when I don't understand English grammar.

Acknowledgement

We encountered the idea of using pictures to elicit feedback from Printha Ellis.

8.7 Somebody else thinks this

Saying what you think without saying it yourself

Language focus   Giving opinions

Level   Intermediate upwards

Materials   Index cards, or small pieces of paper

Procedure

FOR ADULTS AND TEENAGERS

1 Ask learners to write down something they want to say about the course on a fairly small piece of paper (index cards are ideal).
2 Once they have done this, take the cards in, shuffle them and redistribute. Make sure everyone gets a card which they didn't write.
3 Now everyone reads the comments on their card aloud while others listen. You may hear things like:

> I really hate the coursebook.
> I never understand those grammar boxes.
> What I really want to do is learn to speak the language, not do exercises.
> I hated the lesson where we learnt to use a dictionary.

4 After each card is read, pause to allow learners to comment. For example:

> – I don't like this coursebook either. It's old-fashioned and I feel bored every time I open it.
> – I don't love the coursebook but I think it's quite useful to have a book to look at at home.
> – I like the book because it divides the language up into pieces that I can try to learn!

5 When everyone has read their card, and everyone has had a chance to comment, thank learners and ask them to place their card on one of two piles – 'I agree with the statement on the card' or 'I disagree with the statement on the card'. Then collect them in and keep them for your own reference.

Acknowledgement

We learnt a variation of the above on the MA course at Durham.

Variation 1

Proceed with stages 1 and 2 as above. At stage 3, instead of asking for learners to read out, ask them to add a response of their own to the comment on the card and then to hand the card in before they leave class.

Variation 2

Proceed with stages 1 and 2 of the base activity. Learners then pass their card on to someone else who initials the card if they agree with what is written on it and adds a comment if they wish. The card is then, in turn, passed on to the next person who initials/writes. Finally the cards are all returned to the teacher.

Acknowledgement

We learnt Variation 2 from Penny Ur.

8.8 Attitudes to the language you are learning

Expressing how you feel about the target language

Language focus   Explaining reasons for change, or the lack of change

Level   Lower-intermediate upwards

Materials   Board

A version of this activity which can be used near the start of this course can be found at the beginning of the book (Activity 1.10).

Procedure

FOR ADULTS, TEENAGERS AND CHILDREN

Part 1

1 At the beginning of the course, ask learners to draw a series of four concentric circles to make their own personal 'linguagram'. In the centre circle they should write the name of the language they are learning. The circles then represent 'very attractive', 'attractive',

unattractive', and finally 'very unattractive'. They should indicate how they feel about the target language marking a X on the circle that most accurately describes their current attitude to, for example, English.

Part 2

2 At the end of the course, refer learners to these initial linguagrams. Ask them to indicate their feelings about the target language now that the course is over.
3 Now ask learners to discuss their results in small groups of three or four.
4 Finally ask if there have been any big changes and ask learners to say why this has happened.

Variation

If you have used the variation with badges from Activity 1.10, ask learners to make a new badge showing how they feel now, to label it as such and to do a walkabout activity to see whether people's attitudes have changed, and to find out why.

Bibliography

Baudains, R. and Baudains, M. (1990) *Alternatives*, Harlow: Pilgrims Longman.

Cranmer, D. and Laroy, C. (1992) *Musical Openings*, Harlow: Pilgrims Longman.

Davis, P., Garside, B. and Rinvolucri, M. (1998) *Ways of Doing*, Cambridge: Cambridge University Press.

Davis, P. and Rinvolucri, M. (1990) *The Confidence Book*, Harlow: Pilgrims Longman.

Deller, S. (1990) *Lessons from the Learner*, Harlow: Pilgrims Longman.

Frank, C. and Rinvolucri, M. (1984) *Grammar Games*, Oxford: Oxford University Press.

Frank, C., Rinvolucri, M. and Berer, M. (1982) *Challenge to Think*, Oxford: Oxford University Press.

Grundy, P. (1994) *Beginners*, Oxford: Oxford University Press.

Lindstromberg, S. (ed.) (1990) *The Recipe Book*, Harlow: Pilgrims Longman.

Morgan, J. and Rinvolucri, M. (1986) *Vocabulary*, Oxford: Oxford University Press.

Moskowitz, G. (1978) *Caring and Sharing in the Foreign Language Class*, Rowley, MA: Newbury House.

Scharle, A. and Szabó, A. (forthcoming in 2000) *Learner Autonomy*, Cambridge: Cambridge University Press.

Sion, C. (ed.) (1985) *Recipes for Tired Teachers*, Reading, MA: Addison-Wesley.

Index